# The depth of dogs

## by

## katherine able

*all dogs matter*

♥

*Katherine*

**ap** aventine press

Published by Aventine Press
55 East Emerson St.
Chula Vista, CA 91911, USA

www.aventinepress.com

ISBN: 978-1-955162-00-5
Printed in the United States of America

# *Chapter One*

Once upon a time in the land next door, Gerald is watching his minions pack up his home and load his many boxes of belongings into the white moving truck. He's playing a game on his phone but he knows the movers and minions think he's conducting important business. Probably because that's what he told them he was doing when he looked up and thought they weren't moving fast enough, not working as hard as he wanted. He yelled and cussed and called them all a bunch of sorry muthas, and even threatened to kill them. He'd never killed anyone, but he wanted to, they sensed how much the idea of murder appealed to him, and got a move on.

Gerald is moving his base of operations to a remote five thousand acre tree farm. He needs the remoteness because fighting dogs, shooting dogs and torturing dogs makes a whole lot of racket. It has also made him a whole lot of money over the past eight years. In fact, with judicious and skillful investing it had made him a crazy amount of money. Even in silence, his money continues to make money. The scale of operations he'd planned that would make him even more crazy amounts of money required a locale far, far in the country, where the anguished screams and sounds of tearing flesh and breaking bones could not be heard.

The massive barn on the property has been converted into a state of the art fighting venue. The upstairs former hay storage area has been turned into a lounge with a full service bar, an area for betting and gambling, and six concrete block windowless rooms for paid sex. He told Tiny she was on full time now. He made discreet inquiries to find more easy female victims. Last week, he discovered a website where he could buy Asian women and make them his slaves. Though he only spoke English, from a business standpoint it made more sense than hiring local, because with the purchased women he could keep all of the money and make them clean the place as well. He was thinking he could use the chains and collars on them, too, to make sure they couldn't wander off. He'd keep them naked all the time as well.

He looks up from the game on his phone, walks over to the back door, and pulls back the pale curtain. He likes what he sees. What he sees are six piles of money on ship chains securely attached to thick iron rings. Beside the chained piles of money are rotting flea infested shelters with leaking roofs. Three of the chained piles of money begin to scratch in earnest. Because, in actuality, of the six chained piles of money, five are unspayed female pit bulls Gerald uses again and again to create beautiful intelligent puppies who grow up to be slaughtered, one after the other, in terrible violent ways. Each little life went for a minimum of two thousand dollars. Sometimes more. He made money without even trying. Money just seemed to flow into his bank account nonstop.

The sixth chained pile of money is an unnaturally large and fiercely muscled white pit bull. He'd already been bred to the gray and white pile of money. Tonight, he'd have his first fight. Gerald bet fifty thousand dollars on him to win. As for the grey and white chained pile of money, this would be her tenth litter in as many years. And as soon as he could visually confirm that the male made huge strong babies, he'd breed him to the rest.

He'd acquired the male in a trade. He'd traded the old van that had been sitting in his back yard behind the chained piles of money. The van had been used for Tiny, or rather, he'd forced

Tiny to have sex in the van with whomever he chose. But now that he had the venue lined out, he no longer needed the van to make money. Tonight, he'd move Tiny to one of the concrete block sex rooms that looked and felt like a jail cell. The bright primary colors painted on the walls did absolutely nothing to disguise their joyless and sinister purpose.

He knew she thought she would continue to live with him and be his housekeeper, cook and lawn maintenance crew, but the truth was, the sight of her was beginning to disgust him. And the way she never said no to anything he suggested. She's such a loser.

Tiny is standing just to the left of the window whose curtain Gerald has just released. She's smoking another cigarette as she watches her sisters. Petal is almost eleven years old and has no business being pregnant. When Tiny said this to Gerald, she almost lost a tooth. If she hadn't ducked when she did, he would've shattered her jaw. She wonders if she'll ever learn to keep her mouth shut.

She watches Jasmine, Harriet and Brownie scratch, scratch and scratch. If she were allowed to have money she'd go buy flea and tick shampoo and wash her sisters clean and pest free. Poof is smiling at her. She wants to be petted. Poof isn't as bright as the other girls. She hasn't figured out that Tiny only holds and pets them when Gerald is away. She also picks as many fleas off of them as she can, but no matter how many she kills, they seem to continually multiply. Her ankles are continually covered in tiny bites, and swollen, when she must go back inside.

Even though the van was a source of pain and horror for her, she wishes she could've lived in it, to be closer to her family. The one time she'd asked, Gerald had said, "You wanna live in the van, do you?" And he had smiled a smile that conveyed no mirth or life. That night she learned the meaning of the word gang bang and found it difficult to walk for weeks. The bleeding from her backside continued for a month. The van is gone now but the memories taunt her dreams. She looks over at Ruger. The most muscled dog she has ever seen. He stares back at her with sad eyes full of longing. His big chain clinks when he scratches the back of his ear with his left back foot.

Tiny is what her name says she is. She's not quite five feet tall. Her too slender body looks like that of a child. She has mellow brown eyes, one that's a little lazy. She earned that for Gerald when he allowed a sadist to have her for more money than he'd ever made for a two hour session. Fortunately for Tiny, the beating was so severe that it put her out of commission for three months. For three months there was no income or cleaning or cooking or lawn mowing from Tiny. After that, Gerald would permit no one to beat her except himself and since he abhorred physical contact, his brutal efforts were rare, and of course, always her fault.

She looks at Jasmine and senses her anxiety, feels her perpetual discomfort from the millions of fleas crawling all over her body and the constant barrage of flies nipping at her face, ears and eyes. Tiny would run away if she weren't so afraid. She's so afraid. She's afraid all of the time. It takes almost all of her concentration to keep her hand from shaking as she brings the cigarette to her mouth. She gazes at her sisters, Petal, gray with a big splash of white on her chest and belly, Jasmine, black with white on her chest and belly, Harriet, solid black with white tipped toes, Poof, a lovely blue brindle, Brownie, brown with white on her chest and the tip of her tail, and the male, Ruger, who barely possesses a functioning brain from all the inbreeding involved in his creation and arrival. He's solid white and too muscular for his own good. But curiously, he moves with the elegant grace and silence of a cat.

All of the dogs are chained so that they cannot touch. They'd be vicious, stupid beasts if Tiny, over the years, had not secretly petted, held, loved, and named them. They were the only answer to her constant quaking fear. When she was with her family she calmed down and imagined her life disappeared to the point that all that remained was peace, gentleness and trusting agreement. These stolen moments help her retain her sanity and know that there is another side to existence than the one she's living now. Why can't she just leave?!

The blank stare returns to Jasmine's amber eyes and she turns her head away.

The subjugation of Tiny began in the ninth grade when she'd just moved to the small Southern town. On the first day of school she found herself seated in front of Gerald in almost every class. She was new and nervous, and didn't realize Gerald was a burgeoning predator who could instinctively sense the weakest, most exploitable individual in every room.

He quickly pretended to befriend her, especially when he noticed how far behind she was academically. Gerald, unknown to his teachers, was the most intelligent student in the school, if not the entirety of North and South America. He possessed a brain that was truly unique, unique in that no matter the difficulty of the subject, his mind could decipher not only the solutions, but the limitless possibilities. He never missed a day of school, never read any assignments, never opened a book. He just showed up, took the tests and made straight C's in every subject. He'd seen early on that those who excelled were recognized, their families invited to events, photographed, interviewed, and well basically, shown off. The very last thing Gerald wanted was for himself or his family, to be shown off. His mother was twenty-eight years old and looked like his sister. His grandmother, who'd begun pimping out his mother when she turned twelve, was only forty-two, but she too, looked like his sister. In sum, they were a suspicious and unnatural looking trio. Those who came into their orbit paid for services rendered, then left as soon as they could.

His grandmother mercilessly beat him until he was seven years old. That day when she came at him, he picked up her scissors from her sewing bag and stabbed her in the chest, barely missing her heart. No one ever knew of the incident but themselves and the individual paid to mend the wound and shut the f--- up. Satan was alive and grinning in that drab, bloody room that night as the two adversaries, Gerald and his grandmother, stared malevolently back at one another without flinching. His grandmother's gaze promised him extensive physical pain and retribution. His stare promised she'd never get the chance because she didn't have the brains for it. She was somewhat aware of the truth of this, but in the coming years she was to learn in earnest the depth and creativity of her only grandchild's intelligence. Because try as she might to hurt him, humiliate him, damage him or permanently maim him, she never could. He was always fifty steps ahead of her. The Sunday afternoon she tripped and fell down the long flight of stairs in their foyer and paralyzed herself from the waist down, thirteen year old Gerald had looked at her sprawled body from his comfortable seat on the gold velvet sofa. He saw the surprise on her face when she realized he was downstairs. He knew then, as only a despised grandson could, that whatever she had tripped on had been devised for him.

He'd looked at her twisted body and thought it was sheer chance her neck wasn't broken. His grandmother watched him, knowing that he knew this terrible and permanent injury had been meticulously planned for him. She didn't cry out, or beg, or whimper, or ask him for help. But she did turned her face away from his comprehending regard. She would wait for someone else to find her. Gerald had risen from the custom ordered gold velvet sofa, walked down the hall to the kitchen and prepared himself a peanut butter and banana sandwich on whole wheat bread. Then he'd slipped on his worn, too small winter coat and left the house.

Now Gerald is fourteen, sitting behind Tiny and knows he has to find a place to live. Last night his mother informed him that his grandmother had paid human traffickers to take him and do whatever they wanted. "Just get him out of my sight. I never want to lay eyes on him again," she told them as she placed hundred dollar bills, one after another, into tattooed gangster hands. His mother had overheard her mother say this to four villainous and complete strangers. One of the other girls had described the scene of the money exchanging hands.

For the past four months he has helped Tiny with her school work. But, he hasn't actually been helping her, he's been doing all of her work at a grade D+ level, making sure a C- gets in there every now and then, but doing it without ever consulting her. When he proposed the assistance, after spying on her work and confirming her poor skills and lack of education, and watching her, confirming her personality as weak, a follower rather than a doer, someone biddable, lonely, easy to manipulate, he carefully ignored the excitement and gratitude that had lit up her pretty eyes. He was a betrayer from a line of thieves and liars, the sight of innocent and trusting gratitude had made him feel something weird and uncomfortable inside that he didn't like, and suspected would eventually harm him. He had immediately and completely closed himself off from her, just as he had from everyone else. He'd learned too many times that feeling and caring brought only hurt.

He put his plan into action, or rather, his grandmother did. He'd been planning to ask Tiny if he could move in later rather than sooner. Yet now his safety depended on him moving in immediately. He'd thoroughly researched her homescape, discovered rampant apathy, constant inattention, and pathological laziness. It was perfect. Since age seven he'd been stealing money from his mother, his mother's clients, his grandmother, and his grandmother's other three prostitutes in the house, and their clients. He'd acquired quite the nest egg for a boy turning fifteen years old in less than a week.

He had no problem moving into Tiny's home when her family was informed he'd gladly pay for the questionable privilege.

A year later he quit school, encouraged Tiny to do the same, took the GED course and passed with a perfect score for himself and a mediocre, but passing, score for Tiny. He then told her she was going to be his assistant.

Tiny had a cousin who was a minor thug, and heavy into dog fighting. Gerald, who had zero regard for any life form, expressed interest when he learned the cousin had made five thousand dollars over the course of a weekend.

One year later, Tiny can still barely read, Gerald moves them out, and as the years pass, in and out of various homes, until eventually, into the home they're leaving today. He never liked to stay in one place too long. It wasn't until they'd moved far away from her family that Gerald crushed Tiny's dreams and her spirit, telling her she was an idiot, good for only one thing. And that very night, he taught her what it was. It doesn't take eight years to enslave an individual. It only takes one despicable, trust shattering act. An act so vile that when perpetrated upon the victim, robs her of sanity, confidence, and hope. Deep, soul penetrating shame will do this every time.

Tiny is watching Petal lick her growing belly when the old white woman walks into the back yard. At first, she thinks her mind is playing tricks on her, that it's an hallucination. But Tiny has never taken an hallucinogenic or any other drug in her entire life. She doesn't even drink. Gerald forbids it. So she knows there's an actual old white woman standing in Gerald's back yard, leaning on a long wood cane, and staring at her family.

She's wearing a knee length lilac linen tunic over floral patterned leggings. She has shiny black rubber ankle boots on her feet. The dogs look at her and do not react. They don't react because Gerald has beaten, or had someone else, beat and shock them into submission, silence, and stillness, a very long time ago. The new boy, Ruger, doesn't emit even a belch of a bark.

"Ma'am, can I help you?" Tiny asks sarcastically. She's bold with this old white woman, generously showering her with all of the contempt she receives whenever another human being deigns to speak to her. Tiny lives a life absent of choice or power. Now, alone with this elderly stranger, she asserts herself, mimicking the insolent tones she hears whenever anyone addresses her.

The old woman, white hair parted in the middle flowing gently into a long neat braid which trails down the length of her straight her back, turns and stares at Tiny. An endless moment passes before she speaks.

"No, young lady. You cannot. But believe me when I tell you, though it will be difficult to grasp at the onset, I can and will help you."

Tiny puts a trembling hand on the back doorknob. She'll let Gerald handle this. She knows how much he'll enjoy it. Yet she hesitates before opening the door, because the demeanor of this old white woman is different, and truth be told, a little spooky.

Gerald looks up from his texting when the back door closes. He frowns when he sees Tiny come inside empty handed. He can smell the cigarette smoke on her from here. A smell he can't abide, though he tolerates it for some reason. He's about to cuss her out when he notices the excitement on her face.

"Gerald, there's some old white woman out there. In the back yard."

Gerald does not question the integrity or reality of Tiny's statement. She has never lied to him, and knows she never will. He puts his phone on the clean countertop and walks past Tiny to go see exactly what's going on out there.

When he opens the door, he sees the old white woman standing in the middle of the dog area. She's facing him, leaning gently on her cane. She straightens up her when he walks toward her and he sees that she's almost tall as he is.

His plan is to jerk her left arm out of the socket as he drags her to the front yard where he'll throw her on the ground, and maybe kick her in the ribs before returning inside to more phone games and generic texting. However, when he's six feet from her he stops dead in his tracks.

He feels something he hasn't experienced since he was six years old. The old white woman may have a cane, but she's tall, almost six feet, and he can see the muscles in her wrists and legs.

Her faded blue eyes are staring into his light brown eyes. She does not blink. There's something about this old white woman. She is in no way threatening him, but he's paralyzed with fear. He stops breathing when she opens her mouth to speak.

"Young man, you will feel. From this moment on, you will feel everything your companion animals feel. You will feel their pain, their fear, their anxiety and their discomfort. You will feel and smell the filth and squalor in which you force them to exist. If you kill them, you will feel it every year on the day of his or her death for the rest of your life. And if you fight them, you will feel them all. All of them. If you get rid of them, you will still feel. If they're killed by another, you will still feel. If they're abused by another, you will still feel. As of this moment, you are forever connected to these extraordinary creatures you have enslaved and forced into an unnatural state of submission and quietude."

She quickly lifts her cane and Gerald recoils, thinking she's about to strike him down. But she points it at Tiny, who's transfixed by the dramatic scene, and says,

"You will feel her, too. Because you must. Her demeanor is the same as those you have chained and imprisoned here. Any fool can see, she too, is your slave. You will feel her terror, her depression, her anxiety. Any physical experience she has, so too, will you."

Tiny watches in confusion and shock as Gerald does nothing, says nothing, to this old white woman who has trespassed onto his property and addressed him without permission. She looks back and forth from the woman to Gerald, to the woman walking away, to Gerald who's still standing motionless and silent. She watches in disbelief as the woman disappears around the corner of the house, and Gerald still stands in place, doing and saying nothing.

Gerald doesn't turn to watch the old woman leave. He doesn't turn to watch the old woman leave because it's taking the entirety of his concentration to not defecate all over himself. So he stands perfectly still and focuses on the small empty rectangular area where the van sat but is now empty and bereft of life. When he feels he has himself and his bodily functions under control, he turns and goes back into the house.

Tiny has wisely disappeared.

# Chapter 2

One of Gerald's minions is driving The Money Bus to the new venue while Gerald sit in the passenger seat. He can't stop scratching. He has been unable to stop scratching for the past six hours. He has taken three scalding showers and one ice bath. He scratches under his arms, his belly, on his tail bone, between his toes, the backs of his ears, and constantly on his back. He made Tiny examine his naked body thoroughly only to report she could see nothing that would cause him to scratch like this. Nothing has made the stinging stop, and even by using every ounce of his prodigious willpower he hasn't been able to stop scratching. The twitching has become more noticeable as well. He feels like there are millions of microscopic organisms biting him over and over again, all over his body.

Ruger is chained to the wall in the back of The Money Van behind the passenger seat, and he, too, is scratching behind his ears, on his belly and under his armpits. Gerald looks back at him and angrily thinks, "We must have the same thing, man." As he turns back toward the front he pauses halfway, remembering what that old white woman said, and then he shakes his head. He feels jittery and nervous as well, which is unlike him, he attributes it to the rash he's gotten from somewhere. It's the only way he can sanely explain it away.

He tells the minion driving The Money Bus to take the next left. It's a barely visible road, marked inconspicuously by a four foot tall fat blood red iron pole with an inch thin silver reflective strip encircling the top. As The Money Bus travels down the three miles on a remote country road to the venue, Gerald can't stop thinking about that old white woman and what she said. On impulse he calls Tiny. When she answers, he feels afraid for no reason that he can explain. He tells her before she comes out to the venue to go buy flea and tick collars for all of the dogs. When he hangs ups, his anxiety level lowers just a tad. Every inch of his skin stings and burns. Then stings again, unrelenting. His arms are bleeding from the unceasing defensive scratching.

As the venue comes into view he expects to feel a thrill. This was a day he'd been meticulously planning and looking forward to for a very long time. But he feels nothing. Nothing at all.

They leave Ruger in the dark bus and Gerald almost whimpers in fear when he closes the door. Without thinking, he goes around to the back doors, opens them, unchains Ruger and walks him toward the venue. The fear dissipates somewhat.

It looks fantastic. He's standing in the upstairs lounge area, trying to admire the clean lines, the big screen tvs on all of the walls, the perfect bar perfectly stocked, the dark red velvet chairs, and lastly, the completely nude semi attractive Asian and Mexican prostitutes waiting for his approval. But he feels nothing. Flat. Remote. Blank. He walks Ruger over to one of the chains welded to the wall and connects his collar ring to it. He looks down at the dog. The dog looks up at him for the barest moment before quickly looking away. He sits back against the wall, waiting on nothing and no one. Gerald doesn't realize he sighs sadly and deeply at the exact moment Ruger does.

Tiny has stopped at the feed and seed store where she buys the food for her family. It's the one item that Gerald does not begrudge his dogs. He feeds them the best. But it's not as though it were his idea, it's simply because it's Tiny's job to not only clean the house, cook the food, mow the lawn, wash the clothes and cars, and turn tricks, but to feed the dogs as well. One time she'd asked the staff to show her the best dog food in the store. The staff member was a pet lover and loved to talk. She was also, thank goodness for Tiny, extremely knowledgeable about dog food and dog nutrition. She'd shown Tiny the healthiest, most carefully monitored brands and from that moment, that's all she ever bought. Gerald, not understanding or caring about anything dog related, though it was a substantial part of his income, thinks that's what all dog food costs.

The trips to the feed and seed store are one of the few highlights in Tiny's beleaguered life. When she does the grocery shopping she's always accompanied. Not because Gerald feels she'll abscond with the grocery money, or even leave him, she's accompanied because she can't read the grocery list. Thus, she is accompanied so that someone can read it for her. Her trips to the feed and seed store are solo voyages and she looks forward to them because she can wander up and down the pet aisles looking at collars she wishes she could buy for her sisters and, now Ruger, looking at chew toys she knows they would enjoy, and running her calloused palms across soft bedding she wishes they could feel whenever they wished. It's the only time she feels at peace.

She's a regular customer, polite and patient, so the workers are always willing to help her find what she needs and to talk about the five girls and the big boy she pretends are hers, and who are well and lovingly cared for. Here, at the feed and seed store, the love she feels for her family rises up and envelopes her. The friendly assistance of the workers only serves to aid and even prolong the wondrous feeling.

Gerald is on the verge of throwing a bottle of ginger beer across the room when a profound inner peace overcomes him. It's indescribably pleasant, innocent, something he doesn't recall ever experiencing. He stands at the bar, his grip relaxing on the slender neck of the bottle, and thinks someone has drugged him. The invisible rash is still driving him insane, but this relaxed euphoric wave has made him momentarily forget his discomfort. He doesn't move. He fears the feeling will go away if he moves. He thinks that if he has been drugged he'll have his blood checked later tonight before the fights begin, when the staff is checking the blood of the contenders for illegal enhancers or stimulants. A giant upsurge of something marvelous and inexplicable overcomes him and he has to sit down in a bar chair before he falls down.

Tiny has returned to the suburban and is in the back with all of her sisters cuddled around her. She's holding them, petting them, and putting the best flea and tick collars around their big necks as fast as she can. She's grinning and laughing and so happy for them. They're still filthy, and they stink, because they've never been bathed in their lives, but now, at last, the red rashes on their bellies and the incessant scratching will go away. For the first time in their lives they will be flea and tick free. Her joy is infectious and Petal, Jasmine, Harriet, Brownie and Poof lean into her and hug her back. Tiny cries. She cries because by some miracle from heaven, she still can. The million little bites on every inch of exposed skin do not bother her. This love, this returned affection, this mutual adoration makes all the pain go far far away. As it always has. Poof lives up to her name, passing gas as she wiggles her strong sturdy body as close as she can to Tiny's too thin one.

One of Gerald's minions is about to tell him the crowd is beginning to arrive when he notices tears on his boss's face. He slowly backs into the shadows, thinking that he's seeing the beginning of the end. His instincts tell him to leave. Every instinct tells him to leave and go away as fast as he can. For the first time in too many years he never wants to count, he ignores his immobilizing fear of Gerald and creeps silently away into the dark surrounding forest, and he doesn't stop creeping until he's in New York City in black pants, white shirt, black tie and a trim black apron, standing beside a small bistro table asking the attractive older couple if they'd like to start with one of the chef's delicious appetizers because he knows the perfect one to mate with the bottle of Chardonnay they've chosen.

Over the next two hours, as the venue fills with assorted miscreants who've travelled from nearby, and even states away, Gerald is back to his old self. The irritating itching has subsided. He thinks it's because of the salve he made Tiny apply all over his body. By the time the first fight is to begin the urge to scratch has gone entirely. He still has the staff draw some of his blood to test for drugs or anything suspicious.

Beneath the lounge and sex cells Gerald has designed and built a state of the art illegal dog fighting facility. There are four rings for the bouts of terror and death. Two on each end and two rings in the middle. One of his clients owns a thriving construction business and told him about ICF construction. The circles are twenty feet in diameter. The walls are three feet thick solid concrete with enough quality rebar to insure their stability and endurance for five hundred years. The walls of the circles are four feet tall, and without any barrier. One would think that the dogs would try to escape, but they never do. Because they can't. If a dog has the desire to escape, the other dog inevitably has an even stronger desire and drive to kill. When chase becomes a component in a match, that desire to kill is intensified, always to a lethal degree.

There's a triple layer of soundproof insulation in the walls and ceiling. Individuals drinking and laughing at the bar, or raping the enslaved women in the sex cells, will never be able to hear the literal rip roaring brutality downstairs. That is, not unless Gerald taps a button on his phone screen which allows the sound of the violence to be emitted from a top of the line sound system he had installed by another client, who owns a very successful home cinema installation company.

Below, where the arenas are, there are bathrooms, a grooming room, a gambling room, a meeting room, a breeding room, and a keeping room. The keeping room is the largest, and the walls surrounding it are also ICF construction, but only one and half foot thick. The extra effort isn't for security, but so that the dogs in the crates can't hear the screams of the losers. He has discovered it agitates them, and can make for unenthusiastic fighting. He almost put a killing room downstairs as well, but on second thought, to save space, he welded short chains in the shapes of nooses to the surrounding four walls. The losers would be hung until dead. More money could be made while participants bet on the length of time it would take a defeated injured dog to die by hanging, which is actually, suffocation.

If one were to walk along these walls and look at the dead fighters, one would see the scars, butchered ear jobs (which happens when individuals with no surgical skills whatsoever cut a writhing dog's ears without anesthesia), and a surprising number of dogs that looked like they had no business fighting. This is because they didn't. These dogs were taken from the streets, off of Facebook, Craigslist, off of Instagram, because nobody cared. Some were purchased for pennies from shelters that were glad to see them go so that more room could be made for the unending flow of unwanted, unneutered, unspayed companion animals.

One would be surprised to see poodles, golden retrievers, Australian shepherds, red and blue heelers, every type of hound dog, beagles, Yorkies, rat terriers, border collies, Mountain Curs, Treeing Curs, Catahoula Curs, greyhounds, boxers, Great Pyrenees, St. Bernards, German Shepherds, and way too many black dogs hanging from noose shaped chains who were forced to fight when they were born to love and serve, forced to die when all they wanted was to live. The many Chihuahuas and puppies used for bait were thrown in a pile by each arena after they had served their purpose. Illegal dog fighting is an equal opportunity endeavor. Nobody cares who dies, or even lives, as long as it's a bloody, terrifying spectacle and money keeps moving from one hand to another.

At the stroke of ten, Gerald walks over to Ruger. Ruger watches the tall man saunter toward him. He doesn't really know who he is because the man has only touched him to hit him and to speak to him by yelling abrupt monosyllabic orders he doesn't comprehend. He has had four encounters with the man that he can count. He knows he can't count very high, but he knows he can count to four.

The first time was when the man took him from the first place he was. He doesn't remember how long he was in the first place. He spent the vast majority of his time ignored while he was in a crate that was too small, or on a chain that was too short and too heavy. The people there yelled all the time. They yelled when they spoke to one another and they yelled at him whenever they caught him looking at them. He learned how to become invisible in order to protect himself. When the humans came outside or he felt them watching him he would become completely still and never ever look them in the eyes. They always hit him or kicked him when he looked them in the eyes. He knew they were afraid of him but he couldn't understand why. No hand ever caressed or brought comfort to him.

When the little female human pet him for the first time his heart had leapt in his big chest and he could barely stop himself from leaping on her, but he did, because he thought that something crucial to his existence would've died inside of him if he jumped on her and she kicked him after showing him the only kindness he'd ever experienced.

The first time he saw the tall man was when his keeper unchained him and took him to the tall man for a viewing assessment. His keeper put a hand on him to better indicate his muscles and Ruger flinched, expecting a fist. For his instinctual reaction, he was jerked and strangled for a bit.

He'd felt nothing from the tall man. Nothing at all, no interest, no happiness, no peace, no sorrow, only a void of nothingness.

When the mysterious inspection of Ruger was concluded he was loaded into the back of the tall man's van and chained to an interior wall. He had never ridden in a vehicle or walked forward more than ten steps in the entirety of his brief existence. He was terrified. But he did what he always did: stayed completely still and looked down. He knows that's what humans liked best of all.

The second time he had an encounter with the tall man was when the van stopped and the tall man opened the back doors, unhooked his heavy chain and walked him to the back yard of a house. Ruger had never walked on a leash but he knew from too much unpleasant experience, that if he did not go where the human was taking him he would be choked. And choking did not feel good. Not good at all.

In the back yard of the house there were five other dogs chained, but their chains were not as large as his, though just as short. It's the way dogs lived. He was smart enough to know that. They were never supposed to touch another living being ever, in play or love, never supposed to have the warmth of companionship and comfort during cold weather. Never supposed to know joy. Never supposed to know anything really, because that's what forced isolation does. It makes you ignorant of everything. The tall man took him to a spot and hooked his chain to a solid iron rod sticking out of the ground. The other dogs, all female, he knew instantly, looked at him with interest and welcome, not vacant indifference. For some reason, this had made him nervous.

When the tall man opened the back door of the house a little female human had come out. In her hands she carried two large metal dishes. She hip butted the door shut and then stood and stared at him. He automatically looked down. He heard and smelled the little female human walking toward him and he immediately got down on his belly as fast as he could. He stared at the ground, at anything but her. He listened to her quietly place the two large bowls near the rotting building he would sleep in until it fell apart or became so flea infested that the house was affected by it. He stopped breathing when she didn't leave. He thought he knew what was coming but was confused, because all he sensed emanating from her was gentleness, and a deep sorrow.

Ruger, a big boy covered in muscles, yet with ribs far too pronounced and evident, gathered the small amount of courage he possessed and looked over at the little female human who'd squatted down next to him. His eyes met hers at the moment she was placing her hand on his huge head. As her hand gently stroked the bone and muscle, he looked into her eyes and fell in love for the rest of his life.

The third time he encountered the tall man was when he was loaded into The Money Bus. He wanted to pull on the chain, to pull away and run find the little female human. But he had seen the tall man hit her before and was afraid he would do it again. So he acquiesced to everything, willingly sacrificing himself to the whims and nefarious plans of the tall man while fervently hoping he would return once again to her.

And now, here's the fourth time. The tall man is leading him to a black door in the wall. When he opens the door, Ruger becomes afraid. He hears yelling, screaming, growling, barking, the sounds of breaking bones and tearing flesh, and he smells blood. There is so much blood smell. He instinctively tightens his muscles. His heart starts beating rapidly. His breath comes in gasps and he must open his mouth to get air. He doesn't know what's downstairs, but he senses it's terrible, that it will be an awful place to be and that something bad will happen. His bowels loosen in fear.

As Gerald descends the stairs with the dog, he thinks about how he comes from a long line of fighting and winning pit bulls. That he's inbred to the point that all his brain is supposed to think about is killing and breeding. His genetic makeup has been planned and designed to make Gerald a whole lot of money. When he walks down the stairs to the lower floor, he almost grins when he sees hundreds of men yelling and screaming and waving money high in the air, when he sees powerful beasts tearing each other apart, when he sees the dangling bodies of losers along the walls, and finally, when he feels the eyes on his dog, of whom so much is expected. Not for a minute does Gerald doubt that he'll surpass expectations.

But something is wrong. Suddenly in the place of triumph he feels terror. He feels so much terror that he feels his bowels loosen to such an extent that he has to pause in order to exert control. The muscles in his shoulders, back and chest are a riot of spasms. His heart is beating so fast he wonders if he's on the verge of a heart attack. His breath is coming so hard and fast that he must open his mouth to breathe. He thinks that when he learns the identity of the person who drugged him he'll kill him with his bare hands.

Each step that takes him lower increases this unnatural anxiety and fear. He hasn't been afraid since he was seven years old. The thought crosses his mind that this drug would be excellent for anyone who does him wrong or tells him no. Then the tenseness in his muscles becomes so painful he can barely walk. And if he doesn't get this rapid out of control breathing in hand, he's going to pass out. He looks down at the dog and notices nothing amiss. He never truly looks at or considers any of the companion animals he has enslaved and imprisoned in his back yard. But if he did look closely, stopped thinking about his discomfort, he'd notice that Ruger's behavior exactly matches his own. He fails to see Ruger's skin moving spasmodically all over his body. He fails to see his open mouth and the desperate panting, his tail tucked between his legs, and the fearful reluctance that's obvious to anyone with the compassionate, unselfish sense to see.

Ruger is fighting a legend tonight. A grey and white pit bull whose face, shoulders and skin bear witness to his experience while his blank soulless staring eyes indicate the measure of his repeated successes. His name is Stretch. He possesses the crazy ability to stretch and turn his body like a gymnast, but also, he can somehow stretch the muscles of his jaw and get his teeth firmly into the head or neck of another dog, no matter the size. It's a compelling and revolting sight to behold. Stretch is undefeated in his career. Fifty thousand dollars of Gerald's money says this is the night he will die. Stretch doesn't care one way or another. The constant, concentrated brutality in his life has removed the frivolity and indulgence of caring. This is what a life is reduced to when an act of true kindness and compassion is as foreign and unknown as the farthest unseen star.

# Chapter 3

The gate to Ring Three is opened and Gerald enters with Ruger. His eyes are darting around like agitated bugs, but he sees the floor and walls are clean of blood, skin and bones, as well they should be after each fight. He and Ruger watch as Stretch and his owner enter the ring. Gerald feels his knees about to buckle. There's no preliminary folderol in dog fighting. As soon as Stretch's chain is unlinked, so is Ruger's. The dogs are thrown at one another and a senseless gory blood bath erupts.

Before Stretch takes one step forward, a volcano of pain and suffering engulfs Gerald. He feels as though his head is being ripped from his neck. He feels the teeth of a hundred dogs tearing his skin and breaking his ribs. He feels the excruciating suffering of every injured, dying and dead dog on his property. His prodigious mind that has eluded and warped the truth for so long, through the unbearable pain, finally and fully recognizes the new reality the old white woman has bestowed upon him, the justified curse she has exerted upon his life. As Ruger leaps onto Stretch, Gerald feels them all. Experiences everything on a molecular level. So much pain. He screams and screams, and moves and throws and then screams even more. The pain! The anguish! The madness! The pain! The startling insanity and heinous stupidity of it all.

When Gerald comes to, he's on his back in the middle of Ring Three. He has never experienced so much physical pain.

He's wary of moving. He assumes that if he moves the pain will be worse, and worse than this is impossible and sickening to fathom. He dares to turn his head to check his surroundings. He sees the streaks and smears of blood on the concrete wall of the ring. And as he does, his body relives the pain and anguish of all the warriors and victims whose lives have been destroyed this evening. He looks up and wishes he'd done anything but, because the dead dangling bodies of the innocent, the old, the stolen and the uncared for, imprint on his mind and he feels their last thoughts, their confusion, their terror, their pain, and their ability to love. He does not feel their release. No, that wouldn't be the end of the curse the old white woman laid on him. She, a great lover and respecter of animals and humans alike, has only gifted him with the suffering. And suffer he does, until he passes out, only to come to and suffer again, the terrible pattern repeating until he has experienced the tortured lives and deaths of every single canine that came onto his property some while ago.

Tiny is in Gerald's house preparing her sisters' regular evening snack when she hears the gunshots. She stops what she's doing and goes to the door. Her sisters are chained in the back yard Gerald would not fence. They have the same crummy dilapidated shelters. Gerald had looked at her in confusion when she asked him if he wanted her to pick up new houses for them at the feed and seed. When he looked like he was thinking of slapping her, she had turned, saying she'd get the old ones loaded, and she had.

From the kitchen door she watches the barn belch forth humans and dogs alike. She hears an AK-47 firing nonstop from the lower floor of the barn. She imagines Gerald and his cohorts are mass killing the dogs for fun. Then she notices the fear on the men's faces as they run to their cars, trucks, vans and SUVs. The shooting pauses for just a moment before it begins again. Tiny is unafraid. She knows Gerald would never allow her to be killed.

She finishes preparing her sisters' snacks, goes outside to feed, pet and talk to the only company she's allowed. She watches them lap up the nourishing tasty fare. She listens to the clanging of their heavy chains against the metal bowls. She watches them drink the fresh water she keeps supplied near their hovels. She watches them roll on the green grass in the dark, knowing the softness of it will soon disappear into dirt, and that no one will care but her. She goes back inside to make Gerald's bed, and to dust one more time because Gerald can't abide dust.

Tiny awakens at six in the morning, as she does every day. She gets up, goes to the bathroom, then goes to the cupboard for treats. Gerald doesn't get up until noon each day. His lifestyle of crime and other business interests occupy the darkest hours. Tiny is relieved she didn't have to work last night. She's also surprised. Gerald had told her she'd be responsible for cleaning the upstairs and for sex work whenever he wanted her to. She'd made no reply. She had been told so many times that she had no other choice that now, almost a decade later, she's utterly convinced of its truth.

Oddly, the big screen tv isn't on when she walks through the living room. Gerald must have spent the night in one of the sex cells in his new facility. She's glad she didn't. But it's highly unusual for him to do so. He always spends the night in his home. Alone. Tiny is the only woman who has ever spent the night in his house, and not for sex. Gerald has never touched her in that way.

The girls are waiting for her. They look so beautiful sitting and lying down on the lush carpet of green grass. What she wouldn't give to remove the heavy chains and bring them inside with her. She goes to Petal first. She checks her more often than the others. She's so worried this pregnancy will kill her. Almost eleven years old, she's too old to have babies from Ruger. He's three times her size. She caresses her growing belly, then sits on the ground so that Petal can lean against her and be held while she's being petted.

Tiny loves this time of the day. It's quiet, and there is a complete absence of violence. These few hours are the only time she can fully relax. Gerald never wakes before noon so she's allowed six hours of peace and quiet. It's particularly welcome this morning, when her body feels like her own because it wasn't brutalized by strangers the night before. She makes her languorous petting and hugging rounds with her sisters. As she holds each one, she apologizes to them that she can't do more. She checks all of their flea collars and can't help but grin as they look at her without scratching and twitching.

She goes back inside to prepare her coffee breakfast, after which, she'll go clean the facility, check on the other prostitutes, come back to the house to make Gerald's lunch, then stay out of his way as best she can. She fears the freedom she had last night will be paid for in spades this afternoon, and longer still.

She walks across the empty lawn to the facility. The only car she sees is The Money Bus. She doesn't find this amiss. What she does find amiss is the total absence of personnel. Empty Styrofoam cups, candy and sandwich wrappers, empty cigarette packs and half smoked cigars are strewn all over the torn up parking lot. Gerald will have a fit when he sees that. This thought puts a spring in her step and she hustles toward the building to get on with her work. If it looks anything like the parking lot she'll have to work hard to get it cleaned in time to prepare Gerald's lunch. This is the way it must be done. All must be pristine by the time he wakes at noon. If she needs stitches, it'd better be taken care of, if there are drugs visible, they better be put away, if she has trouble walking two steps, she better figure it out. Because if Gerald's house and business is not in pristine order by noon each day, she will and has, paid the awful price.

When she opens the door to the lounge she's shocked by what she sees. There's no way she can get this in order by noon, or even in five days. Broken tables and chairs dot the floor like crumpled skeletons. The mirror behind the bar is gone. There's broken glass from beer, liquor and wine bottles all over the bar and carpet. She looks over at the door to the sex cells and sees it's wide open. She makes her way to it, careful not to step on any jagged glass or splintered wood.

She stands in the doorway and listens, yet she hears nothing. No unsavory sounds, no sarcastic or fake banter, no running showers. No nothing. There's no one here. Just to make sure, she walks down the black lit hall looking into each cell. The mattresses have been slashed apart, and as in the lounge, the furniture has been destroyed.

Tiny walks back down the black lit hall. She checks every room and closet on the second floor. There is no sign of life. As she heads toward the stairs to do something she thought she would never have to do, she sees the four large tip jars are full of money. Now, in a dream like state, she slowly descends step by step, pausing, listening, hoping she'll hear someone or something so that she'll not have to enter and see the horror she knows is on the other side of the solid steel door, that is coming closer and closer.

The door, though extremely heavy, opens silently and smoothly on well-oiled special built hinges. A client of Gerald's built safe rooms for rich paranoid people for a highly lucrative living. He knew exactly how thick the door needed to be to block all sound from downstairs. It's a work of art and precision. Because no matter at which point in the outward swing the individual leaves the door, it stays perfectly balanced, it's crushing weight moving as gently as though it's as light as a feather.

Tiny peers around the edge. The first thing she sees are the bodies of the companion animals dangling from the noose chains. She jerks back in revulsion and vomits on the stairs. So much beautiful life! GONE! She's about to run back up the stairs when she remembers spotting Ruger, sitting in one of the rings. He was, of course, staring at her. She knows he must be hungry. And she must check on him to make sure he's unharmed, and to help him if he is. She breathes in deeply, steels herself, and with the barest hesitant touch the heavy door swings silently open once more.

As she moves toward Ruger she purposefully keeps her eyes averted from the carnage on the walls. He stands and wags his tail when she approaches. There's blood on his mouth, chest and on his right side. She squats down to run her hands over him to check for injury and almost falls over when she sees the dead dog, his throat gone, lying against the far wall of the ring. She shudders. Ruger had won the fight. She hugs him to her, sad that he'd been forced to fight for his life for the mad whims of blood thirsty creatures masquerading as humans, but mostly she hugs him to her because she's so glad that he's alive and apparently unharmed.

Ruger follows her as she trots toward the exit. When they pass Ring Four Tiny sees a human form balled up in a fetal position on the dirt floor. She stops. She holds Ruger back behind her. She looks at the body, tells Ruger to stay and opens the gate that is level with her chest. As she moves forward she sees the man is alive. His breathing is shallow, but he's breathing. As she gets closer, she's stunned to recognize Gerald. It's Gerald, but a Gerald she's never seen before. His face is misshaped, swollen, his jaw is askew. His face is covered in sweat and blood. She can see two wet trails running down his face that can be nothing but tears. He has been sobbing. Tiny, a human being well acquainted with physical pain and profound sorrow, recognizes the aftermath of sobbing when she sees it. It involves every muscle of the body; the work and struggle involved leaves its mark upon the face long after the unbridled convulsions have ended.

She's too afraid to disturb him. She and Ruger leave as quietly as they can.

The day passes and Gerald does not come home. Tiny is by turns terrified and unreasonably defiant. She thinks she has probably gone crazy. For when she and Ruger arrive back at Gerald's, the first thing she does after feeding him is to give him a soapy, filth cleaning bath. Though he's never had a bath in his life, he stands still, staring at her the whole time and letting her have her way. After all, it's Tiny, the first and greatest love of his life. His Tiny, a being filled with love. When she finishes bathing and drying him, she takes him to his spot and chains him to his post, next to his shoddy shelter. But she hesitates before leaving. Then, she stops altogether.

What she does next is the most daring and terrifying act she's ever attempted, though she has endlessly dreamed and fantasized about doing it for years. She moves to Petal, and gently placing her hand on her head, she bends over and unlatches the chain. She then leads her to the water hose and bathes and massages the old girl until she's grinning like a sleepy fool. One after the other, she bathes her dirty, stinking sisters. She cleans their ears. She massages them dry with clean fluffy towels all the while marveling at the beauty of their soft coats. No fleas, no ticks, and no chains. She watches as Ruger, Petal, Jasmine, Harriet, Poof and Brownie smell one another like old long lost friends. She watches as they lie down in the sun, just barely touching one another, but indeed, touching one another.

Tiny is too exhausted and too happy to feel fear. She thinks Gerald will probably beat her to death for these six acts of caring defiance. But looking at her sisters and at Ruger, she can sense how peaceful they are. How lacking in anxiety and loneliness they are. And she doesn't care. She thinks it worth it. When she gets up to go back inside, her family follows her, something they've been wanting to do since the day they were born. And Tiny lets them.

Three more days pass. Gerald remains balled up in a fetal position in Ring Three. No one has come to the house to work, to ask a favor, or to beg for money. It's just been Tiny and her family and the happiest three days of her entire life. Her family is with her all day and all night.

The second day, she'd gone to the facility and hauled out the high dollar dog houses Gerald had purchased for the heavy bettors and winners. They were insulated, large enough for a bed, and to stand up and turn around in. They even had little front deck areas where the dogs could chill, or just stay dry when it rained. She'd burned the rotted shelters and placed the insulated shelters under the two car carport and on the twelve foot deep front porch. When she finished this work, she went to the shed, started the tractor, connected the trailer to it, then gathered the field fencing intended for mothers and puppies, and proceeded to fence an acre around the house. She removed the posts and chains in the back yard and hauled them to the bayou running along one side of the property and dumped them there. After she watched them irretrievably sink to the bottom, she'd turned and discovered her family had followed her, and that they looked worried. But when she yells loud enough to be heard over the purring diesel motor, "It's Ok!", they relax and trot back toward the house. But Tiny, who has not spoken louder than a whisper since she can't remember when, yells "It's OK!" again, then again, and she laughs, and feels all the joy of those receding fat rear ends with those high wagging tails. Laughter! This is what it feels like!

# Chapter 4

Gerald cannot move. He suspects a hip is out of joint, that multiple ribs are broken, that his left arm is broken, that his jaw is shattered, and that he has a bruised spine. He will soon learn that six teeth are gone, four are barely hanging in there, that his right knee and left ankle are broken, his left hip is dislocated and broken in four places, that he has two hairline fractures in his pelvic bone, and that he has a cracked skull. But from the depths of this quagmire of pain, he feels a lightness in his spirit which is utterly foreign to him, and a joy in his heart which he thought had been crushed to dust long ago. He cannot unfold his body yet, but he can feel, above the devastating physical pain, a buoyancy, a joy, that he truly believed only existed in make believe made up worlds on television and in books he once read that he can barely recall.

But it does exist. He can feel it so much that he thinks if he could reach out a hand he'd be able to touch it. His hand would move in the direction of his house because he knows exactly from which this pure bounty emanates: it is Tiny. He knows because across all the years of his beating her and using her and trying to destroy her from the outside in, that there always existed an inextinguishable flame of life. A tiny flame he could never reach and totally, cruelly douse. Try as he might, for some inexplicable reason, a spark of hope dwelled deep within her where no man could reach.

He has no idea what she's been doing while he has lain on the dirt floor of Ring Three. He does know that her joy has been amplified six times over. He can feel the affection and tenderness Tiny and those dogs of his are sharing. For two days, after he woke from the mini coma from the physical torture he'd endured because he no longer believed in the power of wonder and the existence of good, he had felt Tiny's peace and joy and the contentment of those intelligent creatures he'd used but never deigned to name. He feels the struggle in Petal's aged body to nurture the six lives growing in a belly that should've only been filled with food after she gave him the eight perfect beings in her first litter.

He had sobbed. He had sobbed so hard he'd fainted. When he remembers the cause… Three days ago he truly believed that dogs did not and could not think, that they did not feel, that they were incapable of an act as profound and mysterious as love. Now he knows differently. He would look over if he were physically capable of it, to beg those dangling corpses for forgiveness if it would make any difference. For he had felt the trust, the confusion, the love, and the thoughts of every single one. He had felt the emptiness in Stretch, the depression, a sorrow so thorough it had snuffed out all other feeling.

Why had he not seen this? Why do others not see this when it's so obvious? All of those men who came here, none of them believed dogs to be capable of feeling or thought, though they all witnessed time and again, their cries of pain, their cowering in fear, their struggle to breathe and live as they were murdered by a craving for violence that they themselves found incomprehensible. Oh, the terror he had endured! Who was that crazy old white woman? And he chuckles, somehow he chuckles, because it's at that moment that Tiny, on the other side of the property is shouting, "It's Ok!!" over and over again, and he feels her joy as she laughs out loud.

Gerald weeps in shame and regret and hopes with his new heart that Tiny will leave him to die.

On the fifth day, Tiny can no longer bear it. She must go see Gerald. Her sisters and Ruger have become inside dogs. They eat with her, listen to her, go on long walks with her, and then, they sleep with her. There's barely room enough for her in the bed, but there is, because she's tiny.

When she starts walking toward the facility her sisters follow her, but Ruger, for the first time, goes into his insulated house under the carport. She doesn't try to coerce him to come with her because unlike Gerald, who has just recently begun to discern the depth of dogs, she has always possessed the ability. It exists within her to feel, and to know, the suffering of the less fortunate.

Her sisters follow her. Their presence and the hours of the past days have given her a newfound confidence. She doesn't know if it will last, but that at this moment in time as she moves toward the man who has used and abused and terrorized her for almost a decade, it is with her. She looks down at her sisters and sees that they, too, are not afraid.

They enter the facility and walk toward Ring Three. Petal, Poof, and Brownie walk inside the ring and smell Gerald. Harriet and Jasmine see the lifeless bodies of their kind dangling from the noose shaped chains and hesitate. They look at Gerald, at Tiny, they lick her hand to encourage her to leave, but Tiny moves toward him. Harriet and Jasmine leave to sit just outside the open door. They can watch just as well from there.

When Tiny moves around Gerald she sees that Petal is licking his face, that he's alive, and that's he's crying. He looks up at her, then quickly away. Tiny is so startled she almost trips and falls. She doesn't know what to say. Poof is smelling the air and passing gas, but even her superpower cannot cloak the burgeoning smell of decay. Tiny thanks her for her for her efforts as she squats next to Gerald, but far enough away so that his fists cannot reach her. She soon sees she need not have worried. His body, like his soul, is broken and deformed from she knows not what.

On the way back from the hospital, she asks herself why she let him lie on the dirt floor for five days. She tells herself it's because she thought he would come home when he felt like it. He always told her he didn't need her help and to get out whenever she offered it. But he did need her help. She did everything but feed and go to the bathroom for him. He was almost totally reliant on her for managing his home and providing supplemental income. She left him lying on the dirt floor because she just did. She can't figure out why she did it. She just did.

She thinks now is the time she should leave. This is her chance to get away from him forever. But then she looks in the rearview mirror and sees her sisters and Ruger looking back at her, and she stops at the grocery store to stock up.

The doctor had told her they'd be in contact. What the doctor and his staff will eventually discover is that they will not be in contact because it's impossible. The only thing legitimate about her identification was her photo. The number she gave is made up, the address is false, as was her age. They won't be getting in touch with anyone. But when they learned of Gerald's top of the line insurance coverage the questions would soon fade to silence, and to an almost choreographed turning away.

As she hands the checkout girl some of the money taken from one of the tip jars, she briefly wonders what happened to him. It's obvious that his mind is broken along with his body. Who beat him like that? Where was everyone? It was so weird. It's also weird going to the grocery store, buying whatever she fancied and then paying, without anyone looming over her shoulder in a bored, menacing manner.

After the grocery store she goes to the feed and seed and buys what she has been dreaming of buying since she laid eyes on Petal, the first Pit Bull Gerald imprisoned and used. She doesn't bother getting a buggy, she goes straight for the large flat carrier. When she leaves the store it's loaded down with a variety of dog beds, brightly colored food and water bowls, chew toys, balls, treats and more treats, collars that reflect both light and the personalities of each member of her family. They also complement the unique colors of each one.

She buys brushes and combs, extra flea and tick collars, supplements for Petal and her puppies, wonderful smelling efficacious shampoos, canned puppy food, dry puppy food, puppy pads. She buys puppy anything she sees. She buys what she has always wanted to buy for her family but has never been allowed or able to. Her heart soars as she loads the carefully and lovingly chosen goodies into the SUV. Petal, Harriet, Poof, Jasmine, Brownie and Ruger push over and jostle one another to make room. When Ruger barks at the movement all action stops. The girls look at him, startled, anticipating a sharp hard reprimand that never comes. And when Tiny breathes out the breath she was holding, Ruger barks again, causing Tiny to laugh out loud. Tails are wagging and rear ends are moving as she shuts the back doors. As she walks around to the driver's side door she puts her left hand on her mouth to feel her smile.

Gerald is on the operating table weeping uncontrollably. He's overcome by the overwhelming feelings of a type he has never experienced. The surgeons think it's from the pain. If asked, Gerald could not have said or explained it, only that he never wanted it to end. When the anesthesiologist administers the sedative he tells Gerald it's ok. Gerald hears the familiar proclamation and almost smiles a genuine smile. But it has been over sixteen years since he has done so and for the moment, as all fades to black, he tries to remember how to do it.

Four weeks later Petal gives birth to six babies. Three are white like Ruger, but female. One could be Petal's clone but is a male. One is a blue brindle female with white on the tips of her toes and chest. The last, the runt that was born without breath until Tiny filled his lungs with her own, is fragile and must be monitored closely because his siblings shove him out of the way at feeding time. Tiny has to place him next to Petal and remain to watch as he suckles her to make sure he receives the necessary life sustaining nourishment. He's solid black and Tiny can't help but love him the most.

They grow fast, except Emmett. He doesn't begin to thrive until he's four weeks old, at which time Tiny thinks she should've named him TumbleJumble, because he tumbles and jumbles into everyone with never ending abandon and joy. It's as though he's making up for lost time. Petal, understandably, is worn out with them and doesn't want to nurse. So at the four week mark, Tiny separates them from her. While everyone, except Petal and her babies, was at the vet being spayed and neutered, she purchased a portable fencing apparatus specifically designed to sequester puppies, baby ducks, baby chickens, baby anything really. It's set up in the living room and puppy pads cover the floor beneath it.

Tiny is exhausted, but happy for the first time she can ever remember. She loves caring for everyone. She loves how relaxed and content her family is. She loves that Jasmine is wearing a yellow collar with pink flowers on it, that Harriet's is red with blue and white dancing bears, that Poof's is brown with purple and red balls on it, that Brownie's is gold and can be seen in the dark, that Ruger's is black with American flags waving in synchronicity around it. She loves that Petal's is black patent leather and that from it hangs a red heart with her name engraved upon it. In big capital letters, just like everyone else's.

She's exhausted from the work, the cleaning, the constant cleaning, and the tending. But she's not exhausted from the affection and love. These abused and neglected companion animals love her so deeply, and it's with a humble wonder that Tiny returns the love, and probably for the first time in her life experiences what it means to be loved and to love deeply in return. She's not ashamed to admit how much she cares for these creatures, whom she has had the privilege of watching bloom and thrive under her care and newfound freedom.

She looks at Ruger now, lying on the floor while Emmett crawls all over him and chews on his ears and his mouth. She watches Ruger fall asleep while Emmett works him over, and she thinks that Ruger is not a fighter and was never meant to live such a demeaning life. He's gentle, patient, and a remarkable daddy to his offspring.

What makes humans think they can do whatever they wish to creatures other than themselves? What gives them the right to use and destroy lives whose value, even to this day, is proving to be invaluable to humans? How can humans be such idiots? Any fool has got to know that chaining an animal or forcing them to live in a chain link cell is wrong. Their misery is obvious to anyone who has a brain and eyes to see. Why do so many humans allow this disrespectful treatment? It's so wrong, yet it's everywhere. Can't people just think while they see? Is that too much to ask of her fellow man? It must be. She thinks, and shudders when she remembers how she has been treated. How insane for her to think speechless creatures would be given more consideration? Haven't the past years educated her to the awful reality of humanity? She ought to go get a gun and shoot them all and then herself. But she can't! Why can't she? Why can't she give up?

The true miracle, which Tiny can't see after years of betrayal, misery and abuse heaped upon her by her fellow man, is that she has not given up on them or herself. Tiny is one of the rarest creatures on earth. She is one who is incapable of hate or being the deliberate source of distress to another living being. The years may have been mostly malignant, but the unpleasantness has not, and will never, penetrate her heart and soul.

If she could only shake the fear. The fear that keeps her from leaving, the fear that makes her stay. She looks down at her family and wonders where else she could be with them. She has no job, no money for a long term arrangement, can't read and has no legitimate identification. She's trapped.

In the first weeks these crushing feelings of being trapped almost suffocated her. But as each day unfolds into the next and peace continues to reign, she disciplines herself to live in the moment. She couldn't worry about something that may never happen. She begins to believe that she is a survivor and can survive. What could be worse than what she has already lived? So after a while, Tiny relaxes.

She removes all of the money from the tip jars and puts it in a kitchen drawer. It fills a one by two foot drawer to the brim. In order to make it all fit she has to smooth out the bills and stack them neatly side by side. What she can't fit using this manner, she puts inside a shoe box. When the shoebox is empty, she fills it with money from the drawer. The shoebox has been filled two times. Dog food, treats, shampoo, toys, flea and tick medications for twelve dogs – it adds up quickly.

By the end of two months her discipline pays off. She no longer worries or frets about tomorrow. Instead, she embraces the long heat filled days and spends every waking moment with the dogs. Ruger goes everywhere with her because he'll have a raucous throw down fit if he doesn't. The first time she left him to go to The Facility he barked, then whined, then rolled on the ground, then convinced her his back right hip was dislocated. His hysterical cries were effective. The sight of him dragging his bottom across the living room floor in seeming agony scared her to death. The sight of him recovering immediately when she opened the gate for him made her smile.

She and Ruger are exploring the land today. They have walked and walked and have encountered no other person. She hasn't even seen another house. Five thousand acres must be a large piece of land. Within the vast virgin forests she discovers trails that men must have developed when they planted and nurtured the trees. They wind throughout the undulating terrain. She crosses running streams, wades through clear water creeks. She sees fallen giants taken over by the flora and fauna of the land. She and Ruger sit beneath the shade of a huge fallen pine tree to watch the ants, the squirrels, birds and an armadillo congregating and working. Tiny breathes in deeply, unaware her spirit is healing as quickly as her body.

On the way home she begins to trot. When Ruger passes in front of her she speeds up and runs. Then runs faster, racing Ruger all the way home. Winded and out of breath, she falls down on the lush grass. Her sisters and the puppies run out to greet her and to make sure she's all right. Once they're confident she's ok, they flop down beside her, near her, or on her.

Tiny looks up at a beautiful blue sun brightened sky. The dogs are chewing on bones or balls or rope toys. The puppies are climbing over her legs and stomach and she thinks how wonderful their little warm healthy bodies feel. She watches bright white clouds move gently across the sky. No two clouds alike, she thinks. She plays a game with herself she remembers from her adolescence, Find Something. For her, all of the clouds are dogs or dog related. She sees running dogs, jumping dogs, grinning dogs, sitting dogs, all different breeds.

A perfect breeze blows across her face. She reaches her hands up to the sky and the bright sun. She looks at her hands. There are callouses from work and scars from injuries. She sees the veins, the outlines of her bones through her flesh.

She looks at her hands, flexes them against the clouds, stretches them in front of the sun, and decides they are good hands. They are hands that have helped heal wounds, deliver healthy puppies, comfort the anxious and lonely, hands that have cooked delicious nutritious meals for both dog and human alike, dexterous hands that have mended clothes to prolong their use, cleaned many a room, polished many a window and bathroom floor. She looks at her hands and decides they've done a good bit of honorable work. She thinks, then believes, that her hands are an extension of her mind and heart. That her hands have completed good tasks and worked for good. Maybe the tasks were menial, but the jobs they completed were important to the puppy who lived, to the dog covered in fleas, and to the people who cleaned their plates. What Gerald forced her to do with her body, the way he permitted others to abuse her, that was not her doing. Those were not her ideas, and the vile acts perpetrated upon her had nothing at all to do with her or who she was.

Ruger has been staring at her unceasingly from three feet away. Now he shakes off his offspring crawling on top of him, lifts his big muscular body and goes to the tiny human he loves with his whole heart. He licks away the water soaking her cheeks. He licks her neck until only his slobber remains. He puts his big head on her chest to stop her trembling. Birds sing enticingly to seek out one another. Strong winds move through the tops of the tall pine trees and they bend without breaking.

Tiny sighs deeply as she places her small honorable shaking hands on Ruger's massive head and rubs him gently behind the ears. A peace filled calmness comes over her. Something has changed inside her, deep inside, in the place she has kept hidden and forgotten, until now.

# *Chapter 5*

Months pass. Tiny, Ruger, and whomever of her sisters can keep up, run up and down the trails in the acres of the untouched forest. There are acres upon acres of pine trees that soar into the sky, their trunks so big it would take all of her sisters touching nose to tail to encircle the biggest ones. The birds sing to her and one another. Tiny will pause from time to time to listen. This has become a time of slowing down. Slowing her thoughts, trying to learn wise thinking. Though she is running more than she ever has in her life, the pace of her life is in slow motion, and she likes the gentle feel of it. She hopes the newfound peace in her life will help her discover the right direction to move toward. She has admitted that a vast change, a shift of tectonic proportions is occurring in her life. She has no idea what she wants, she only knows what she will no longer allow. This time of solitude is calming her spirit and giving her confidence. She'll never forget the value of solitude.

When Tiny was a little girl she loved to run more than anything. Not wild racing down the streets and sidewalks, just even paced nonstop running. When other children were playing in the neighborhood playgrounds and nearby abandoned homes, Tiny was running. She could run fast if pressed, and she was sometimes, because there were, and are, always predators waiting, hoping, and plotting to prey upon the weak and the too trusting, but most of the time Tiny just jogged.

She could outrun them all if need be. She could skyrocket forward and maintain her speed until she ran into something, tripped, or nothing. She had never run out of breath and no one had ever caught her because she was as coordinated as she was fleet of foot. She could dart and dash with startling speed out of the reaching grasps of those who meant to harm her. She didn't curse them or think about them. They were just a part of her life. Adults attempting to prey upon her had started in her own home when she was five years old. Horny sick uncles, horny stupid teenaged boys, and then the man who said he was her father but never acted like it. No one ever caught her. No one ever caught her until she trusted and ran toward the one who convinced her of his good intentions simply by never attempting to touch her or make her feel that he desired to do so.

When she started running again she forgot about smoking. The habit just completely evaporated.

She's running through the forest. Ruger runs beside her, in front and behind. He may pause from time to time to investigate something interesting, but he never lets her get farther than his sight. They run. Ruger never needed to acclimate his weird body to the long runs. Tiny's muscles eventually remembered the rhythms, although the years of chain smoking initially crippled her. At first, she was easily winded and even vomited when she pushed herself too hard. But those days are gone. Tiny runs for hours each day. When it rains, she runs. She runs at dawn. She runs at midnight. She'd run twenty four hours a day if she could, if she didn't think it an exhibition of unhinged behavior. Of someone running from something.

The running cleanses her. Her now healthy body becomes pure muscle. Her lungs become stronger, too, because she practices using them wisely, breathing in and out deeply, and with conviction and purpose. It takes so many hours, so many days,

days that melt into weeks, then months, but soon she realizes her mind has become as fit as her body. By the end of five months, she has spread her sorrow, her anger, her self loathing and her anguished memories along the pine straw strewn trails where they were further trampled by many paws, until they were light enough to float into the limbs of the trees where they were decimated by the grabbing branches and sometimes aggressive winds. But try as she might, she cannot totally rid herself of the fear she feels for Gerald.

Again and again, she asks herself, why doesn't she leave? He could be dead for all she knows. But she knows he isn't. Somehow she knows. Her main excuse is the dogs. There are twelve dogs under her care. Twelve dogs who depend on her for food, care and affection. The thought of selling Petal's puppies does not even occur to her. It never would.

At night in the living room, after hours of running, after activity spent playing with the puppies, after cooking, feeding, petting, bathing and simply sharing being alive together, Tiny sits on the sofa with Emmett in her lap and Ruger at her feet, the others on the floor or on their beds or on the other furniture, and thinks about her future. What she's supposed to do. Sooner or later, the money will run out. She can't read. She has no legitimate identification. And she's not a criminal, a person who can go out and unconscionably steal, cheat or lie. What does that person do with her life? What can the person who has no money and no skills do? All she knows is dogs. That's all she knows how to do.

She thinks these thoughts without realizing that she does have skills. She can manage a household, plan menus and execute them, landscape an entire yard with imagination and keep it manicured to perfection. Tiny has so long heard what a loser she is that she secretly, almost wholeheartedly, believes it. What stops her from believing it is the unconditional love she's exposed to every day, all day long. There are twelve perfect souls who look at her with love and believe she can do anything. When she's with them, she thinks everything might just turn out ok.

It's six months to the day when her family warns her of an approaching sound. She's behind The Facility, putting wildflowers on top of a grave. Her family is inside the fence, even Ruger, because none of them like to come here. She goes inside The Facility and puts the bucket back in the storage area. The dogs can't see her and neither can the people pulling up to the front of the house in the silver sedan.

The dogs are barking to warn, protect, welcome and to invite to play. The puppies are running around the older dogs as they bravely sound the alarm for this unprecedented occurrence. The puppies are nipping, fat, happy and joy filled. Loved. They have never known a chain. Never known human inflicted brutality. Tiny raises a steady hand to her perspiring brow and wipes the moisture away. She knows exactly who it is.

This day was inevitable. And now she must make a choice. She wipes her palms on the front of her jeans as she looks toward the house, the home she has made. The lawn is lush green. The windows sparkle because she keeps them crystal clear. She sees the dog houses and elevated dog beds scattered on the front porch and under the carport. She see chew toys, brightly colored balls, old running shoes chewed away to almost nothing. In her mind she sees her bedroom, the kitchen, the living room. Thick, soft dog beds along the edges of the rooms. Soft piles of blankets dot the floor like little friendly hills. Bags of carefully chosen treats are on the kitchen counter. She sees the only safe and comfortable place she has ever known. A place she has transformed into a haven of warmth, security and freedom. Her family has known freedom.

Tiny feels her heart begin to pound and the muscles in her legs begin to quiver. She memorizes the sight of Ruger barking, of Emmett tackling his siblings, of her sisters, Petal, Jasmine, Harriet, Brownie and Poof standing at the fence with their tails wagging and wagging. Her sisters she has set free and cannot bear to see imprisoned again.

She watches Gerald exit the sedan with the assistance of the driver. He's using a cane and looks weak as he stands. She watches the sedan drive off. Gerald continues to stand with his back to her. She watches him looking at her family. She watches the dogs reactions. The puppies are overjoyed as they have only known kindness from humans. But Tiny is surprised to see her sisters are not afraid of him. She sees that Ruger has stopped barking but he, too, does not appear to be afraid of Gerald. She doesn't understand what this means.

Gerald turns his head and stares into the shadows of The Facility because he knows that's where Tiny is. He can feel her. He knows she's watching him. He wills her to come forward and meet the man he is becoming. Come out, Tiny, come out.

With one last glance at Ruger, to make sure he's not looking for her, she silently fades into the shadows of The Facility. When she comes to the open back door, she's already running as fast as she can. Running away from the man who beat and enslaved her, running away from a life to which she can never return, running away from the only love and loyalty she has ever known. Her mouth is wide with a scream Tiny will not allow to exit. She runs, and runs, and runs.

Gerald feels her moving rapidly away and he can do nothing. He looks down at the scene before him and has to grit his teeth not to cry. He has cried seven oceans in the past months. In the past two weeks he has seared onto his brain the words he will to say to Tiny. Now that he's here, facing the joy and contentment he has only experienced from his hospital bed, he cannot speak. He looks at these magnificent creatures he tried to destroy and sees before him their complete rehabilitation. Where once they were silent and hunched in filth and endless boredom, he looks now into eyes shining with intelligence, warmth and trust. He looks at their beautiful healthy bodies and is ashamed he made no contribution to their current wellbeing. The feelings are overwhelming because he can *see* everyone now, and because he knows each and every one better than he knows himself.

He knows that Ruger always wants to eat. That Jasmine likes being scratched behind her ears, that Harriet likes belly rubs, that Brownie will wait her turn with perfect manners, that Poof passes gas only when everyone is nearby and can smell the officious bouquet she'll proudly admit as her own. He knows Emmett is special to Tiny. That he almost died and if it hadn't been for her tireless loving ministrations, he would have. He knows that Petal is tired and having a difficult time bouncing back from her last forced pregnancy. What he doesn't know is, other than Emmett, which puppy is which. He knows their names as well as his own, but while he can feel everything they feel, and even at times listen to what they say to one another – he doesn't know who is who.

As he feels Tiny moving farther and farther away, he looks at the companion animals in his manicured yard, the ones he chained, shocked and ignored in the back yard of wherever he lived. He shudders when he thinks of the hovels they lived in, the lack of care he gave to these remarkable intelligent creatures, creatures capable of problem solving, of coexisting without fighting, of watching out for one another and their human family. He thought this would be one of the most perfect moments of his life. His homecoming. But to his horror, what's actually happening is that he's filled to the brim with nauseating self-revulsion as image after image flies across his mind in ultra high definition of every second of every act of cruelty and neglect he bestowed upon these amazing beings.

From a physical standpoint, the first month in the hospital was pure torture. The wounds and injuries to his body were numerous and profound. He had no explanation because he had no idea, at that time, how it happened. And his broken jaw, broken arm and fingers prevented him from any type of communication. His right eye had a detached retina and the left side of his face was heavily bandaged due to it almost being ripped off by something, these injuries and their necessary coverings prevented him from communicating with his eyes for two weeks. It wasn't until a month later that he was fully apprised of the extent of his injuries, injuries he was never be able to explain to himself or the attending physicians as to how they were received.

He signed all of the permission forms for elective plastic surgeries. They told him when he'd likely be released but warn him that it will be a year or two before he has fully recuperated. He made no remark as he handed the last signed form to the hospital administrator. She had returned his health insurance card to the table by his bed and complimented him on the amount and levels of coverage his policies provide. He closed his eyes and ignored her, recalling how he would brag to himself and his minions not to worry about health insurance because he had enough coverage for them all.

His body is sliced and stitched, and then sliced and stitched even more. He eats through a straw for weeks. He does not speak to anyone. Nor does he thank anyone for their assistance, time and care of him. They watch him wipe tears from his face and tell the doctors, for God's sake, get him on antidepressants. But the doctors shake their heads and say he has refused all medication. He will only allow the anesthesia for the surgeries.

One day Gerald wakes up crying again. This time he feels no frustration or shame. He reaches once more for the box of tissues he keeps on his bed that cost him two hundred and fifty dollars and pulls one from the box to slowly wipe away his tears. He has experienced the birth of Petal's puppies. He has felt the weakness and will to survive of Emmett. He feels the relaxed state of Tiny's family, now realizing his dogs were her family. He is awakened to the realization of what family means. Something Tiny and the Pit Bulls could've taught him over and over again if only he had not held them in such hate filled contempt.

And so he becomes a legend. The nurses, PAs, LPNs, physical therapists, nurse practitioners, doctors and surgeons think that the silent crying is from the intense physical pain he's experiencing every second of every day. They accept his conversational absence because they believe his pain prohibits him from speaking. They don't know why he has forbidden any medication. But because it's his right, they must comply. If the doctors say do it, what choice do they have.

What they don't know and will never know, is that Gerald is only vaguely aware of his physical discomfort. He uses all of his energy and intellect to focus, and to stay focused, on Tiny and his dogs. It soon becomes more of a habit than an effort.

He sleeps and dreams Tiny's dreams. He learns the feeding schedule so that he can eat when everyone eats and fully experience the pleasure and taste of food.

Month two finds him lucid and convinced of his predicament. He's no longer in denial as to the reality and truth of the old white woman's curse. He begins training himself to become more aware of Tiny and his dogs.

The doctors are dumbfounded by the rate of his recovery. He doesn't respond to their remarks and questions because it would make no sense to them. They'd never understand that the power of love is healing him. Never would they believe it for a second. So he remains silent, yet all day every day, he wills his mind to stay with Tiny and his dogs. The twenty-four hours that make and bind a day are filled to the brim with an all-encompassing love that exists in her mysterious relationship and connection with his dogs. It engulfs him, embraces him, and slowly but surely not only heals him, but changes him.

It's during month three of his convalescence and recovery that Gerald begins to understand what it means to be a human being, and the enormous responsibility that accompanies this realization. He feels Tiny and her family, but differently now. It's not with the confusion and disbelief of the first month, or the greedy mental love grabbing he engaged in in the second month.

Month three finds him relaxed and thinking of the life he will now have with Tiny and her family. He wants very much to be a part of what they have. He wants to be in their lives but he wonders if they can bear to have him in theirs.

Gerald is a man who, before this time, did not believe in love. He had been taught that it was a physical act that only took place when two people were naked, grunting, and rolling all over one another. How could he help but think this? It was the lie of the environment in which he was reared. Make love this way, make love that way. Now he knows that there was no love in the home of his mother. He realizes she had him so that she could have a friend, but her mother, his grandmother, crushed that idea as quickly as it arrived. As soon as his mother finished nursing him, his grandmother put her to work and supplied the drugs that would forever tether her to an ignominious existence.

The question which continues to confuse him is, why don't people love? It's so much easier and a whole lot less complicated than violence or manipulation. He knows that an act of true love is one that isn't physical. It may compel one to touch or hug the one loved, but the state of nudity and rolling around on one another is the farthest thing from love that there ever was.

For his entire life Gerald has abstained from all physical contact, except for the violence he doled out. The lovemaking he grew up watching, and then sold for a side income, had nothing whatsoever to do with love. It was a base act committed and sought after by unthinking, and ultimately, unfeeling humans. The only thing human about them was the shape of their forms and the appearance of their skin.

Because of the so called lovemaking Gerald witnessed during the formative years of his life, he vowed to remain celibate. He is a virgin, and thinks he'll probably remain one until he dies. He's relieved to know he can still pursue love to learn what it means.

It's as though a secret door has been opened and miraculously, he has not only been given permission, but feels this tremendous invisible encouragement to walk through it and into a real life. He now knows that's what love is – the realest, most genuine reality.

# Chapter 6

Gerald is standing in front of the gate when he feels the intense adrenaline surge of Tiny. He uses the burst of energy and strength to quickly open the gate, lumber clumsily inside, and then close it. He turns and looks for her, tries to find her slender form racing through the forest. Because she's racing, racing as though she's escaping mad roaring flames that seek to grab and destroy her, racing away from him as fast as she can.

He looks and searches until he's sure he cannot glimpse her. He's turning back toward the house when Snowbell, Cotton and Silky jump on his legs.

He feels himself falling in slow motion. Petal and Ruger's solid white babies think he's coming down to play and help as much as they can to aid his descent. When he falls onto the soft grass all of the puppies except Emmett run to lick his face, sit on his shoulders or to stand on his stomach and crotch. They're hurting him, but no dog has ever been allowed such liberties and access. He concentrates on their joy and affection rather than his discomfort. He can feel not only every ounce of their weight, but also the exact measure of their happiness and curiosity.

He can't get over how large they are at five months of age. Even the females. For the first time in his life he extends a hand to a dog without intending violence or cruelty. He runs his hands over any puppy that will let him. He feels their delight in response to human touch. He feels their remarkably soft coats which they inherited from Petal. As he caresses and studies the puppies, Petal, Brownie, Jasmine, Harriet and Poof move closer to investigate. He sees that their tails are gently wagging.

Gerald feels a dog nudge his head, then softly lick his forehead. He looks up into the steady gaze of Petal, his premiere breeder. He can't even remember how many puppies he has gotten off of her, and sold to anyone who could pay his exorbitant prices. Now, as she comes around to lies down beside him she continues to look him in the eyes and he notices her eyes are brown with flecks of golden amber, and that they are on him, warmly filled with patience, waiting to see what he'll do next.

Gerald knows what he would've done in the not too distant past if a dog ever looked him in the eyes. Unpleasant, painful and demeaning repercussions would've been sure to follow. But now, he lifts his left arm to invite Petal to come closer to him, and she does. She lies close next to him and puts her head on his shoulder, all the while looking into his eyes.

"I'm sorry, Petal. I'm sorry for the way I treated you, for not naming you, for using you again and again to fatten my bank account and increase my reputation among the standing of terrible men. I'm sorry, Petal. It won't happen again."

Petal looks at him, slowly blinking her eyes as though she has understood every word and concept he has uttered. The truth is, she has already forgiven him. Immediately after every injustice, every cruel, tormented act that was visited upon her by Gerald, she forgave him. A being filled with love and trust has no room or understanding of anger or spite or revenge. With her eyes closed, she sighs deeply into his face and Gerald smells breath that is healthy and true. He moves his left hand to the top of Petal's head and gently pets her. He feels calmness and contentment radiate through him, just as much as he feels the stressed unceasing exertions of Tiny as she runs farther and farther away.

As the puppies settle themselves on and around Gerald, he wonders about love. He's not a man of illusions, he knows full well that he does not love these dogs, however, he respects and admires them. He wants to share the bond with them that Tiny has. How does one love? How is it done? What is the procedure, the protocol? What's the first step?

As the sun bears down on his tired body these thoughts and meanderings cascade through his mind. His last thought before falling asleep is that Ruger and Emmett have made no attempt to come near him. They stay away and never stop staring at him. Ruger only seeing a monster, and no Tiny.

Tiny will never know that Gerald was apologizing to Petal over and over again. She will never know that Gerald was going to apologize to her in a clumsy, unpracticed, but sincere fashion. She will never know that Gerald was on the verge of giving her the greatest gift she never asked for. Because her brain remembers the pain he caused so vividly that her body reacts as though it's happening all over again. She wants to scream a great loud warning to her family but she cannot. And she couldn't stay and watch him do to them what he did to the others. Her feet fly across the earth as they never have before. She is strong yet afraid, more confident yet bereft. Tiny moves and the wind seems to aid in her escape. She doesn't know where she's going, only that it takes every ounce of her willpower to not look back.

Later, Gerald awakens and attempts to rise, but one of the fat fine puppies steps perfectly on the sorest point of his healing broken leg. The searing pain takes his breath away. Rather than react with a heavy hand, he holds his breath and waits until the pain is bearable. Then he gently moves a gorgeous but dangerously energetic blue brindle Pit Bull puppy from off of his leg. He notices her dangling red heart shaped tag reads LOLLY and that she's looking at him with expectation. It's an expectation he will not betray. He looks back into her gaze and hopes that some of the wonder in her eyes will one day be transferred to his.

He slowly rises from the ground using his cane. When he's standing, the adult females and the puppies run toward the house. He looks over and sees Ruger and Emmet staring at him.

"Ruger, I wouldn't want anything to do with me either. I wouldn't get near me. Emmett, you're right to trust your daddy. I had terrible, uncaring plans for him, and for you, too."

Ruger looks at Gerald, then turns away and walks to the fence to stare at The Facility. Emmet doesn't move. He continues staring at Gerald.

Gerald looks at Emmett, really looks at him. Not just seeing, but with consideration and honest interest. He can see that Emmett has taken after Ruger in all ways except color. Emmett is solid, glistening black. Gerald can tell he will be huge like Ruger and have the same pronounced musculature. And like Ruger, he's silent as a cat. The only thing he can see that he got from Petal are her sweet eyes. He hopes he got her intelligence as well. He's ashamed of himself for focusing only on strength, speed and viciousness when breeding dogs in order to obtain a specimen like Ruger. He notices that Ruger has been neutered, and he's glad of this. He assumes Petal, Jasmine, Harriet, Poof and Brownie have been spayed. He wonders if he'll be able to feel that, too.

He limps nearer to Ruger. Ruger does not look back at him. Gerald senses his distrust and total lack of fear. Gerald thinks that the lack of fear is a byproduct of constant love, affection and care. He also thinks that love, affection and care must be confidence builders. He feels no threat from Ruger. What will he feel once Ruger realizes Tiny isn't coming back?

"Ruger, you're right not to trust me. To ignore me. But, but, I want you to know that I'm sorry for what I did to you and as long as you live, you will never be subjected to such ignorant treatment. I will never harm you again and I won't let anyone else harm you. I'm sorry for what I forced you to do. I'm sorry for the way I treated you. I'm going to do better from now on. I will learn how to do better, Ruger."

Ruger continues to stare at The Facility. He raises his mighty head and sniffs the air. He can still smell Tiny almost twelve miles away, a smell that's moving in the opposite direction from where he is. Gerald swears he sees Ruger's shoulders dip a little, as if in defeat. But it's not that at all. Ruger is exhaling so that he can breathe in deeply, as deeply as he can manage, so that what he does next will be strong, forceful, and heard. Ruger lifts his chin and emits a howl of such sorrow, such longing, such beckoning that it chills Gerald to his bones. He wishes he could comfort him but knows now is not the time. A foundation of trust must be built, and then built upon.

He limps toward the house and the dogs waiting for him on the front porch. Emmett watches him. He looks over at his father howling as loud and as long as he can for the tiny human who does not appear. He watches the tall limping human moving slowly toward his home. Emmett is a puppy and curious, and sensing no threat, he runs after, then passes the human who will now feed and be a companion to him. The human who will take care of him. Because isn't that what humans do?

RUGER STAYED by the fence for five days without moving. His eyes, mind and body pointed toward the direction he last saw Tiny go, the direction where her scent wafted no longer. Gerald has left him alone. When he didn't come inside to eat the first night, he took food and water to him. Each morning everyone went outside to do their business and to go eat the food Ruger had not touched. Emmett would run to his father, smell him, lick his unmoving face, sit for a minute, then drink water from his bowl.

Gerald has fully recognized and admitted to himself that he knows absolutely nothing about dogs. He'll keep his mouth shut and his hands to himself, unless they ask him to touch him. He doesn't feel natural petting them without an invitation. The past five days have been spent watching dog videos and walking back and forth to the window and standing on the front porch to check on Ruger. He has ambled near him a time or two but he felt like he was intruding. There has been no reaction or movement from Ruger. There is no profitable information online about helping a dog whose heart is broken.

On the fifth day, Gerald is awakened at four o'clock in the morning with puppy licking and breathing. When he opens his eyes Brownie puts a paw on his arm and pulls it toward her. He also smells the deliberate pungent aroma of Poof's superpower. He hears open mouthed panting from the eleven dogs crowded into his room. The puppies go in and out of his bedroom; the adult females have never crossed the threshold. Something is wrong.

When he throws back the covers and turns on the lights he discovers everyone is crowded near his bed, all eyes wide in alarm and panting abnormally. Brownie continues to paw at his hand. Emmett is panting hardest of all. Gerald feels the distress from him and the adult females the most. He's sleepy and confused until… Ruger! He can barely feel Ruger!

He gets up as quickly as he can manage, and barefoot, moves toward the front door. When he opens the door the dogs bolt through it and run towards the fence. When he thinks how they could've left via the pet door but chose not to, he becomes even more concerned and quickens his pace as best he can. He jog walks to the spot where Ruger has been planted for five days. Ruger is no longer there.

Emmett and his siblings have begun barking and yipping excitedly by the gate. Gerald can make out the agitated white forms of Snowball, Cotton and Silky. He wills himself to move faster and when he's almost to the gate he sees the collapsed form of Ruger, lying motionless on the grass.

Now that Gerald has seen Ruger, the puppies quiet down and move slightly away as he bends over their sire. Gerald kneels beside him, putting one hand on his ribs and the other on his neck. Ruger is alive. For how much longer, he doesn't know. He feels the confusion and profound sadness emanating from the big dog, but he's truly shocked as he grasps the depth of his despondency. Ruger has lost the will to live. The absence of Tiny is defeating him, killing him.

If Gerald had not seen and felt this tragedy first hand, he never would've believed it. If someone had tried to describe this scene to him he would've called him a liar and an idiot. If someone had tried to tell him that dogs worry, mourn and become depressed, he never ever would have believed it. Yet again, he berates himself for his callousness, for his blindness, for his idiotic lack of insight, when all along, for years, the evidence of their complexity had been right in front of him. But he had chosen not to see anything because of a bone deep selfishness which consumed his every waking moment.

He knows he can't carry Ruger all the way to the house. His strength has yet to fully return. He jog walks back to the house and gets the wire mesh wagon that's underneath the carport. He's pulling it away from the house when he hears Jasmine bark sharply at him. Yes, he now knows the distinctive barks and noises of each and every companion animal. When he looks back toward her he sees her head lower and her teeth grab one of the cushions from an elevated bed. He understands immediately.

Now as he pulls the wagon toward Ruger there are two soft cotton pads covering the hard wire bottom. When he's pulling Ruger back toward the house he's interested to see and feel that everyone has calmed down. They're not only depending on him to revive their kin, they have full confidence in him that he can do it, that he knows all the answers. Gerald considers this as he wheels the wagon into the middle of the kitchen. When he turns around he sees all of the dogs surrounding the wagon in a U formation and looking up at him expectantly.

"I'm not going to let you down," he says to them, and the comedic truth and wonder of the moment strikes him. He has spoken more honestly to dogs in the past five days than he has spoken truth in his entire life. Is he becoming a man, or just slowly metamorphosing into the human being he was intended to be?

He won't let them down. He walks to the freezer and removes the biggest cut of meat he can find. He unwraps it, and after consulting his phone for instructions, he puts it on a plate in the microwave to thaw. He brings an elevated bed into the kitchen and gently lifts an unconscious Ruger from the wagon to the bed. Ruger does not move a hair. Everyone is quietly watching him. It's four thirty in the morning. The perfect time for a snack. He opens the cabinet doors and pulls out bags of treats and generously dispenses them while feeling the weight of tremendous responsibility on his shoulders.

As he feeds them the treats he also feeds them praise. At first, it's awkward because he has never praised anyone or anything, not even himself. But as he recalls how they woke him up and communicated to him that something was perilously wrong, and how they led him unerringly to the scene of peril, the praise begins to fall easily from his lips because he's genuinely amazed and impressed by their most definitely praiseworthy actions. He watches them happily chew delicious treats chosen by another.

Dogs! They're so smart and multifaceted. As he looks at each one while he waits for the meat to thaw, he thinks about how they're utterly unique in appearance. Even Snowball, Cotton and Silky are easy to tell apart. He has learned they each have different dispositions and personalities. That they are helpers. That they are confidantes. He has seen how sensitive and loyal they are to their brethren and humans alike. Each dog, each who was specifically bred and raised to kill, destroy or reproduce, as he watches each dog gently take the proffered treat from his hands he can't help but think that the world is upside down. The world is deaf and blind to all that is good and life affirming. How does this happen and why is it so prevalent?

When the microwave dings he turns to fetch a cast iron skillet from a dust free well organized drawer. He places it on one of the eyes of the clean gas range. The fire comes to life immediately. When the skillet is hot he places the thick slab of beef on it and is rewarded with sizzling sounds of cooking. Once the meat is brown and crusty on both sides he slices it into small bite sized pieces. He looks back at Ruger and sees no reaction. He mutters to himself, "a dog mourning the loss of his human so deeply he was starving himself."

Gerald stirs the meat around in the skillet until it's well coated with the liquid fat. He turns off the range and moves the skillet to a cold eye. He turns around to look at Ruger. No movement. The other dogs, satiated by the unaccustomed bounty of treats at the irregular hour, are dozing on the floor, elevated beds and furniture. Gerald looks at the relaxed scene before him and to his astonishment says out loud, " I wouldn't have it any other way." The truth of the surprise utterance sits well in his newly awakening spirit.

When the meat has cooled enough to touch, he takes one of the larger pieces, dips it in the juices and then gently rubs the moist meat around the edges of Ruger's mouth. Then, morsel of meat in hand, he stands up and waits. He hopes that what he learned about Ruger's appetite while he was lying in the hospital bed serves him well now. He remembers the incredible appetite he has, how it seemed that Ruger was always ready to eat. He waits.

His wait is rewarded by the sight of the tip of Ruger's tongue moving out and around his mouth to lick away the appetizing greasy moisture on it. When his tongue flicks out again, Gerald quickly puts the morsel of meat on it and is gratified to see Ruger take the food and swallow it.

He grabs the skillet from the stove and puts it on the ceramic tile floor near Ruger. He sits on the floor and for an hour, slowly feeds the depressed dog the food he needs to survive.

# Chapter 7

Gerald is awakened at seven o'clock in the morning by a wet tongue on his mouth and the smell of puppy breath in his nostrils. In the four weeks since he has returned, much has changed in his life. His schedule being one of the many big adjustments. Gone are the days of staying up all night and sleeping until noon or beyond. His new schedule, or rather, his schedule according to the dogs, is up at six thirty or seven and to bed by ten or before. Though some nights he can't sleep due to the lingering discomfort.

He hasn't seen or heard from Tiny. He has felt her, though. She's somewhere working hard. He feels her deep exhausted sleep in the evenings and the long hours of industry during the day. He wishes she could feel what he feels, see what he sees, and know what he knows. Every day is a revelation. That's what love is, he knows now. There's no bottom to love and one can never get enough of it.

He has enthusiastically embraced the responsibility of caring for Tiny's family; he has admitted and fully acknowledged that the dogs are hers. He's trying to take care of them for her as she took care of them. He recognizes that she took care of them not for him, but for them, because they're living breathing, thinking, feeling, sensing creatures who deserve care and attention. Man, has he come a long way! Every single day he's humbled by their total forgiveness of him. It's as though they only remember who he is now.

It has taken longer for Ruger to come around. Emmett tried to remain standoffish, but it went against the grain of his personality. He's a happy go lucky loving fellow and affection is the bread of his life. Gerald is learning patience from Ruger. Ruger is also teaching him how to be kind, sincerely kind.

This morning he's deep within the acreage of his forest. Everyone is with him and everyone can keep up. While Gerald is recovering and becoming stronger each day, he still can't stand on his feet for hours a day. Even Petal, the oldest and most easily fatigued, comes on these relaxed walks and enjoys it.

The heartbreak and shock of Tiny's leaving continues to wear on Ruger. He'll run, sniff and act interested in all that's around him but Gerald knows that what he's doing is seeking the presence, the smell of Tiny. He still doesn't come too close to Gerald. He sleeps in Tiny's room on her bed, and Emmett and Day, Petal's male clone, will sleep there with him most nights. Ruger is eating, not as much as he used to, but he's eating.

Gerald doesn't doubt that Tiny will return. And when she does, he wants her to know that, in spite of him, she took excellent care of her family. He'd had no idea what or how to feed them. He'd found the food and treats but was so ignorant of the process that he didn't know which was which. Online research solved that dilemma.

As he waits for Tiny's return he learns as much as he can about companion animals. Initially, he did it because he had to, but soon he does it because he wants to, the more he researches and reads about dogs, the more he wants to know, and then because when he's not with them or watching them, verifying the research, he finds himself fascinated by the subject and the subject matter. Though Gerald may be changing in some ways, his mind is as it was before – alive and interested and most at ease when it's fully engaged in learning or figuring something out. He learns that companion animals need exercise. He knows his body does as well if complete healing is to be achieved. Thus, long walks two times a day with the young begin to take place, and then, also twice daily, he takes short intellectually engaging walks with the elders. His reading has revealed that dogs need mental stimulation just like humans. And after seeing the behavior of Ruger, he'll never doubt the intelligence of dogs ever again. And Ruger is the least intelligent of them all!

For the girls he used as breeding machines, he has devised short trails that push them both physically and mentally. Petal is the brightest and most gung ho of The Lady Team, as he has taken to calling them. She thinks she can go on long walks, but one trial outing and her distressed wheezing had convinced him she couldn't and shouldn't. He felt her enthusiasm at the same time as he felt the stress of the exertions on her joints, muscles, lungs and heart. He knows a major cause of her inability to walk and run as much as she wants to is because he kept her on a six foot chain from the day he got her when she was seven weeks old until her age of eleven now. He knows he was her jailer and the author of her enslavement and all suffering. Some days when she looks up at him with her tail wagging, her tongue lolling out of her mouth, and her bright eyes gazing into his with adoration and trust, he must look away from her as flesh crawling shame engulfs his body and mind.

He didn't know that companion animals thrive on affection, human attention and touch. He feels the pleasure and delight every time Petal, and all of the females he mistreated, see him. He doesn't know if it's because they sense the drastic change in him or if because they've been free to roam for almost seven months, because they know freedom and true care. Her genuine and unflagging interest in him is confounding. She wants to be with him all the time. He finds himself reaching down to pet her more and more often. She has wrapped him around her paw and he'd have it no other way. Who would've thought he could be endlessly fascinated by the maturation and behavior of Petal's last litter? He wishes Tiny could know that he'll have her spayed next week, and will do the same for her puppies when they reach the right age. He wishes Tiny knew that Petal and her offspring are being cared for in the proper manner, that he would never chain them again, or make them live outside if they don't want to. Most of all he wishes he knew where Tiny was, her exact geographic location.

He can feel her fatigue, her anxiety. Her loneliness. He knows she cries every night as she falls asleep because she desperately misses her family. At times he can feel her embarrassment. He wonders what that could possibly be about, then realizes someone has asked her to read something. Then her embarrassment becomes his shame.

His shame then forces him to remember how he treated her, what he made her do, so that he could have some pocket money. How is it possible that a person, once so despicable can then somehow not be? Despicable. Despised. That's what his grandmother called him when no one else could hear – Gerald The Despised. Gerald, whom nobody cared about, Gerald, the little boy who was born to be despised. What a lie.

Right now the last thing he feels is despised. He feels wanted, treasured. He thinks he'd feel this even if there weren't eleven dogs showing him kindness, attention and affection every day. He believes that the love that Tiny has inside her, that is now inside him, this love is there whether or not any one or any companion animal is around to physically demonstrate it. This mysterious and endlessly generous thing called love is available and in never ending supply to anyone who will accept it. And it doesn't come from humans. It comes from somewhere else. He doesn't know where, only that the supplier is bigger and more powerful than any gun or rapacious mob, or other malignant evil. When a person can acknowledge love and accept it, it will erase confusion and illuminate the world.

He knows he must go to The Facility to give the remains of the slaughtered innocents a proper burial. Today is the first day he feels he possesses the necessary physical and mental strength to complete the gruesome task. He leaves the gate open and isn't surprised to see that no one follows him. No one passes past the gate. Not even Ruger. Even the dogs know it's a place unfit for the living, and especially unfit for the pure of spirit. He doesn't beat himself up any more. Gerald has accepted that he has changed, he's embracing it, and to live in the past in a constant state of beating himself up serves no purpose. What's done is done. It was awful what he did. He has the rest of his life to make it right and he's determined and on the path to do just that.

He hesitates when he comes to the door. He looks back and sees Ruger, Emmett and Day are sitting on the porch watching him. The rest of the dogs are lying on the ground just inside the fence line. The scene and silent support fortify him. He turns back to the door, opens it wide, and steps inside.

He looks along the back wall where he expects to find the rotting corpses of all the animals he had a direct hand in slaughtering. The metal nooses are empty; the bodies are gone. All that remains is dried blood and strands of fur in rough circles at the base of each spot. He looks toward the ring where he forced Ruger to kill. He looks at the ring where he endured his torment. A wave of deep emotion overcomes him causing him to stagger. He puts his hand on the wall for support.

The moment he touches the wall all of the death and destruction of that day washes over him. It's not as intense or as crippling as it was, but again, he feels the pain and confusion of the companion animals who were robbed of life and love on that day.

This curse the old white lady bestowed upon him is terrible. Part of him wishes it would end, while another part of him couldn't bear to see it depart. The experience of feeling so much horror that he directly caused hurts him, steadily hurts him, but also, it's healing him. There's nothing he can do for the dogs that are gone and respectfully buried by Tiny buried in a neat row behind The Facility.

He could tear the place down. A part of him wants it razed to the ground in the hopes that the memories will be razed from his mind as well. But he knows it wouldn't be so easy. The new Gerald is incapable of erasing unpleasant memories of atrocious acts dealt by his hands or orders. As he walks past small grave after small grave he thinks it's a part of the changing. The graves run in double rows from one end of The Facility to the other end. The little graves force him to remember the puppies and toy breed dogs he slaughtered. Some are medium sized graves that make him remember the Foxhounds, Heelers and Basset hounds he slaughtered. Some are large sized graves that make him remember the St. Bernards, Mastiffs, Bloodhounds, Great Danes and Pit Bulls he slaughtered.

He knows he can discipline his mind to forget the face and fur of each dog, but as he stands looking down the rows of graves Tiny dug, and probably then gently filled, he makes himself recall the face and eyes of every single dog he saw that day. He will not give himself a pass on that day. If he is to continue to learn about this mystery called love then he must learn to love truth most of all.

He walks back into The Facility he turned from a barn that nurtured life into a vicious hole of violence and death. If Tiny can bury dogs and make them sacred, he can turn on a hose and begin the long hard work of removing the traces of evil. And hope that as he washes it away, whatever evil remains in him will be washed out, too.

TWO WEEKS LATER Gerald is gliding down the long driveway in one of the silent golf carts he'd purchased for the valets. He's driving to the mailbox to pick up the weekly food delivery. When he left his grandmother's house he no longer had to cook for himself, though he still remembers how to do it, and that it was one of the few enjoyable acts of his youth. As his body completes his healing, he has reinterested himself in cooking. The recipes, simple at first, have become more and more complex. Yesterday he enrolled in a cooking master class. Maybe he'll be a chef. Since he wants to be home when Tiny returns, he never leaves the grounds. He orders all food and supplies online. He even orders toilet paper online. He orders everything online because he won't leave. He wants to be here when Tiny comes back.

When he arrives at the end, or beginning, of his driveway, he sees all of the packages are neatly stacked beside the oversized mailbox, instead of inside it. He climbs down from the golf cart and opens the gate while Petal, Harriet, Poof, Jasmine and Brownie wait for him. The Lady Team enjoys riding in the golf cart so he takes them each day down the three mile length of driveway to the mailbox. Petal and Jasmine are in the front seat with him. Poof was at first, but the ride always excited her bowels and Gerald couldn't take the constant smell of her excitement. She rides in the back seat with Brownie and Harriet. He didn't allow the puppies or Ruger to follow them because he doesn't trust Ruger to not bolt. Ruger constantly seeks Tiny out, and one day last week he ran away and was gone a full twenty four hours. Gerald doesn't want to think about Tiny's sorrow if he loses Ruger, or any of them.

He unlocks and swings open the heavy duty iron gate. Taking care of the dogs and the regular walks in the forest have eliminated the need for the cane. He's getting stronger every day and no longer is there an unnatural tilt to his long stride.

He notices the mailbox is open, which is unusual. He becomes immediately suspicious, because that part of him is a forever thing. He remembers with clarity what he did with a machine gun not too long ago, nasty reprisals wouldn't surprise him. As he nears it and is able to peer inside, he sees the bottom half of a shoebox sitting all alone in the big metal box. He pauses and listens, yet hears nothing. He moves nearer and is able to see inside the box. Someone has abandoned four recently born tawny striped kittens.

He gazes at them with new Gerald eyes. After a few moments of considering the evidently breathing thumb sized forms, the terrible thought crosses his mind that the old Gerald would've carried them across the deserted country road and thrown them into the bayou without hesitation. Maybe even watched them struggle and sink. But new Gerald gently takes the box, hurries back through the gate, locks it and drives back to the house as fast as the cart will go. The box is cradled securely on his lap.

The Lady Team is adroitly weaving on the cushioned bench seats and grinning in appreciation at the feeling of the wind moving through their open mouths and across their bright eyed faces. He looks over at them, sees the joy in their eyes, feels the joy in their spirits, and when Petal and Jasmine glance at him, he grins back at them, because thanks to the old white woman, their joy is his as well. He's now convinced that a Pit Bull mouth was designed to grin. Not kill. Not harm. He looks back at Harriet, Brownie and Poof and all three girls look at him as if on cue. The adoration and trust in their eyes in undeniable. He winks at them and faces forward.

He has learned it doesn't take  much to please the dogs as long as the dogs can be with him. That's what they desire most of all. To be with him, the past author and perpetrator of all misery in their lives, yet now, the provider of too many treats, the eager companion of long walks, golf cart rides, and affection whenever they wish.

He has learned that he, too, was not designed to harm, because kindness comes so effortlessly. There's no need for planning or manipulation or covert machinations. Kindness is natural and the first instinct in the face of like kindness. To betray kindness takes dark effort, and that darkness is not all transferred to the victim. It stays, festers, and grows like a kudzu vine, covering everything in its path, until light is hidden in the one who acts with thoughtless cruelty. But though the light may be forgotten and become a foreign thing, it's there. It's never completely extinguished. It only takes the gentle action of pushing away the ever encroaching shadows through consistent acts of unselfishness, and awareness of what one can become if pervasive carelessness becomes a way of life.

The dogs want to be with him and Gerald wants to be with them. He wants to see them, pet them, look at them and please them. Not only because he can feel their pleasure, but because feeling their pleasure has become not only pure delight, but also a reckoning. He'll be glad when he can share pleasure with Tiny's family without the instant accompanying unpleasant slideshow of his past actions. He wonders if it will ever cease. Then new Gerald thinks it'll be ok, he can take the unpleasantness as long as his life continues to overflow with these days and nights of indescribable and potent revelation.

Yesterday, he took The Lady Team to the lake located along the southern edge of his property. He was curious about something. When he pulled the golf cart up to the bank of the body of water no one got down until he did. When he walked to the edge of the water, they followed, and like him, stood looking across the wide calm expanse of it. When he waded into the water they watched him with worry and fascination. His body was vanishing but the human was not distressed. When only his head was showing he began calling the girls to him. All but one ignored his invitation. The one who constantly surprises him with her intelligence, generosity and courage.

Petal began to slowly wade into the water. When the water was at her belly she stopped. The rest of the girls sat down on their haunches to watch the mystery unfold.

Gerald waited and watched her, quietly coaxing her toward him. She looked down at the water and at the disappearance of her legs, then back up at him. He continued to call her to him. Then not taking her eyes from his face, she moved deeper into the lake. When her feet could no longer touch the muddy bottom he saw and felt her confusion and panic. So he moved forward and gently took her into his arms. He felt her begin to relax. He could feel the water moving gently against her body and her panic rapidly subsiding.

He continued to cradle her in his arms as he moved farther away from the shore. Petal licked the water, and then his shoulder. When he thought he had reached the right distance, he hugged her to him, kissed her wet muzzle and was rewarded by a warm feeling of relaxation from her.

He had sensed her calm, her curiosity, and her complete trust in him. How many times must he accept Petal's pardon until he can forgive himself? He's been hugging and kissing dogs! The very same dogs he was convinced had no brains or sensory perceptions. As he held Petal in his arms he'd looked back at the rest of The Lady Team on the bank of the lake. He felt no ill will from them. It was as though they have forgotten his moral crimes. When will he forget them? Can he ever forget them?

All of Petal's muscles were slack as she gave herself over to his embrace as though it were the most natural and safest place in the world. He'd turned slowly around in the water. With his hands on her chest and abdomen he'd held her out and moved her as though she were being pulled behind a boat. Even when he'd gone faster she'd not been concerned. Her slow heart beat went thump thump thump, never changing its placid pace.

Then he'd pushed her toward the shore, walking beside her as she swam. Her body relaxing and enjoying the way the water moved around her and held her up, but most of all, she enjoying the presence of the human who remained less than an arm's length away, and who she knew would not let her come to harm.

She had looked toward the shore. When the gooey bottom met her paws she'd she walked out, acting as though she had been swimming all of her life and not for just the past two minutes. Gerald moved back into the water and watched in amazement as all of The Lady Team walked into the water to swim toward him. He felt the water on their bodies and the pleasure they felt at their weightlessness. He felt the comfort they derived from the water, too. When they reached him, he moved away toward the shore. They had followed.

The rest of that afternoon had been spent watching The Lady Team become confident swimmers while ensconced against a back drop of tall healthy green trees and blooming wildflowers. Butterflies and bees fed on the bounty undisturbed by Gerald's energetic throwing, again and again, of the right sized sticks into the lake for them to fetch. And he couldn't help but laugh at the trail of bubbles that followed Poof wherever she swam.

The laughter is a sweet undeserved balm as he's acutely aware of Tiny's fatigue, stress and worry as much as he's aware of the calm joy that surrounds him. He searches for her every day, but to no avail.

The activities of that afternoon had solved a puzzle and answered a question to which he suspected he already knew the answer. He can not only feel their emotions and the directions of their thoughts, he can feel every sensory experience they have. He wondered about this one day when he felt hungry after just finishing a satisfying meal. It wasn't his hunger he felt, it was Emmett's. The question came to him again when Snowball and Cotton rubbed against his leg. It felt good to him, but he didn't know if he was feeling their pleasure or his. Now, he's quite sure of the depth and complexity of their shared connection. But is it just with them?

# Chapter 8

When Gerald arrives back at the house he places the kitten filled shoebox onto the kitchen counter. With his right index finger he lightly touches each kitten to confirm body temperature. Immediately after touching them, he can feel everything they feel. They're alive and healthy, but need food right away. They're very hungry and very confused.

Gerald searches through the kitchen, pantry and storage to gather sustenance for one day. After that, they'll require food for their specific age and breed related needs. As he prepares their temporary fare, he orders proper food and has it overnighted to the mailbox.

He can feel their body temperatures dropping.

He trots into his bedroom and opens the closet door to his well-ordered space. As he reaches toward the shelf where the folded heating pad lays he hesitates, and accidentally notices the perfect dust free order of his closet.

After Tiny left, he hadn't known what to do. He'd never been alone in his life and he didn't want to be alone now, especially with all of the inexplicable changes occurring and evolving. He'd moped around like a two hundred year old man, from the wounds, crippling loneliness and full time self pity. The physical injuries would take time to heal, but the loneliness, how did one go about curing that?

The dogs had sensed his fragility and watched him carefully, with Ruger watching him closest of all. Gerald was keenly aware of the unhappy feelings of Ruger. He knows he betrayed him while Ruger thought they were family. He feels Ruger staring at him and trying to comprehend why he would feed him, and then try to kill him.

He begins to see things from Ruger's point of view, from all of their points of view. He learned it's a point of view that has more sanity in it than most humans possess. The dogs' needs are simple, and except for seeking companionship and food, they're without ambition. And so they are peace filled, pretty much all of the time. The only time their natural way of living and existing is altered is when humans interfere, to use them for selfish and unseemly pursuits. Yet they quietly bear the burden of neglect and abuse, but when presented with the opportunity to experience generosity and true consideration they melt into it and recover as though nothing unpleasant had ever been systematically visited upon them for years.

From his comfortable chair on the front porch, Gerald spends a large portion of his convalescence watching the dogs, studying the behavior of the dogs, feeding the dogs, then petting and caring for the dogs, and always, always, willing Tiny to come home.

Now, as he walks back into the kitchen with the neatly folded fresh smelling heating pad, he looks at his house. And he remembers.

His living room lacks the order and cleanliness Tiny imposed upon it. He remembers every day when he got up at noon or one o'clock, the house was spotless, his clothes were clean, the dogs were fed, and his brunch would be on the way, and without fail, absolutely delicious.

He remembers watching her mow the yard. In his degenerate perversity he'd never let her grow a vegetable garden. Why did he refuse that request? She would've grown the best vegetables in the state. Everything she put her hand to she did with diligence and excellence. He knows there's nothing she can't do if she is of a mind to.

The new Gerald will tell her his. But is it even conceivable that after almost a decade of insults, browbeating and abuse heaped upon her by old Gerald, that the positive words and support of new Gerald will be accepted and trusted? He has to believe they will. He has to convince her of their truth and apologize for all of his lies and mistreatment. He will! He will! If only she will come home.

He remembers the day after she left. He was disconsolately standing in the kitchen eating a pitiful ham sandwich while watching the dogs eat. He'd found the huge pot of dog stew in the refrigerator. The laundry room freezer was stocked full of ten pound bags of leg quarters, bags of diced carrot and peas, broccoli florets and clear ziplocs filled with small cubes of sweet potatoes. He knew it wasn't for Tiny, and that no one else had been here, so it was all for the dogs.

He'd found all of the food, the different types, some for older dogs, arthritic dogs, puppies, for active dogs, for dogs like Poof with digestive issues. He had a mind numbing amount of time on his hands so he read and memorized the ingredient list on each bag of anything dog related. After researching every single ingredient and then cross checking, he had admitted to himself that he was impressed. Tiny, who couldn't even read, had chosen nutritious fare for physical and mental development. How had she managed that? With the close tabs he kept on her? Because love prevailed, always found a way.

He'd looked at the dogs then, really looked at them and saw how good they looked, how healthy they were. He knew it wasn't due to any action or thought on his part. It was all her doing. She loved these dogs like a family, and had taken the best care of them that she possibly could, or as much as the idiot Gerald would allow.

He'd watched Petal turn and stumble, and he'd felt a sharp shooting pain in his left shoulder. Her arthritis was flaring bad that day. He'd put down his pitiful sandwich, turned toward the cupboard and taken down the bottle of supplements that would ease her pain. He molded a pill pocket around it, then watched as she gently took it from him in gratitude. Petal, the sweet girl he'd forced to live in her own waste, to be covered in fleas, to be filthy, and he had worn out her body to the point of almost killing her by forcing her to have litter after litter, non stop, Petal had gently licked the hand hanging by his side, then maneuvered the same hand until it was on her head in a petting position.

As he'd looked down into her brown and amber eyes, he'd felt the kindness of her spirit wash over him, and once again, for the ten millionth time, he felt the tears fall. It confused him to no end how he could've been so blind to the depth and mystery of these creatures. He doesn't understand how he could not have seen it, noticed it, when all over the world the intelligence, the versatility, and the skills they possess are constantly on display in stories telling of the bravery and loyalty of dogs, in blockbuster films and television shows devoted to dogs, dog themed toys, clothes, the list never ended of examples illustrating the extraordinary attributes of this companion animal. How can this creature be so respected yet held in such contempt? How did he not see who and what they are?

Was it simply because they can't speak using a human language that they're so disdained? He had held them in such contempt that he truly believed they didn't feel, much less think. Why was that? Generational curse? Or by only coming into contact with others who thought the same? His mind had sped through and examined each and every one of his contacts until he was awash in revulsion. What was wrong with him? Why was he like that? Why didn't he see, really see, the horrible people he surrounded himself with?

He knows the answer. Ruger tells him every time he looks up at him. He was an evil beast filled with evil thoughts which led to evil actions and deeds. His former life was consumed with preying on others with no concern as to the suffering it caused. He now understands that his former existence was a form of insanity. A madness. His arrogance and anger had turned his heart to stone and blinded him.

Through Ruger's eyes he sees the fighting circle, and as Ruger looks up, Gerald sees the rage, the mental derangement, the screaming, the yelling, the money changing hands, the fists pumping the air, the red faces, the wild eyes, the spittle spewing from the uncontrolled shouting. He's in Ruger's mind feeling the doubt. These creatures are supposed to care for him. But terror and death have nothing to do with caring.

Gerald had closed his eyes against the incessant flowing images. In that not long ago life, he ran after only what could serve him, benefit him. And the quicker, the better. He hadn't for an instant considered how he could serve. He'd viewed servitude as worse than a curse.

So much time, so many years wasted. And what was the actual bounty of his reign of terror? He had no friends, knew no joy or peace, never felt comfort. Never felt relaxed.

Here though, an undeserved second chance. A second chance, and mountains of cash. But what can money do for a man who is ignorant, ashamed and tortured by his past? His new insight into companion animals has not only fully awakened him to the mystery and fragility of existence, it has made him vulnerable because he genuinely cares about something and someone other than himself. He wants Ruger to trust him and like him. He wants to be a comfort to Petal and ensure her remaining years are easy.

He wants to learn what life is about. Because he knows it isn't about money and domination. That it's a terrible distraction that misleads those participating in horrendous acts far away from reality. He understands how short sighted a life filled with nothing but destruction is. Because inevitably and without doubt, the destroyer is destroyed as well.

When he reenters the kitchen to take care of the kittens, he sees the dogs, except for Ruger, are sitting in a semi-circle in front of him. They're watching him, waiting for the new adventure that this human introduces into their lives on a daily basis. And something smells interesting on the kitchen counter. They wait for Gerald to introduce them to it, or to indicate the proper behavior regarding it.

Their eyes are trust filled, confident, and steadily gazing into his. There's no looking away, or down, in fear, or in an impossible attempt to become invisible. They've wholly accepted this human as their friend and ally. They're all together in this mess called life, and by supporting one another, it makes figuring it out and quotidian living a lot more manageable.

What does he have on the countertop in that box that he finds so compelling? Is it food? Because a lot of food happens in this room exactly on the spot where the box is. Quietly, and with the patient curiosity of the happy and well loved, they watch and wait.

Gerald moves to the counter to plug in the heating pad he'll use to warm the kittens. Then he slowly lifts the kittens in order to place the heating pad and a clean folded towel beneath them. The pad warms quickly.

He mixes the food together in the blender until it's a thin runny liquid. He barely heats some of it on the stove, and then, with the plastic syringe he begins feeding each kitten. He can feel their thumb sized bodies accepting the nourishment. It takes no time at all to fill their miniscule bellies. With the heating pad becoming the perfect temperature, soon all four of the newborns the are sleeping. He stands over them and watches their tiny chests move up and down in a life affirming rhythm. He touches the heating pad eight more times before he's assured they won't be burned and they won't be cold.

They'll live. He knows they will because he senses nothing other than hunger bothers their systems. If he will feed them, they will live. If he will hold them in the cushioned palm of his hand while he feeds them, they will thrive. If he cherishes them as they grow, they will develop distinct personalities and their intelligence levels will flourish. If he gives them a stable and consistent home environment, they will love him until their days end.

Gerald considers this. The first creature on earth who will truly love him will be a cat. His cat. His cats.

He must give them suitable names. Names that will not demean them. Names that, with every utterance, will undeniably indicate more about the character of the owner than the character of the pet. Names that are appropriate and fitting. Something they will come to when called, and something that will give him pleasure when calling.

He decides to call them The Qat Quartet. He names them Quentin, Quincy, Quantum and Qani. Three boys, one girl. He is Gerald, pet owner and nurse maid. First time actually engaged pet parent, and inept namer of companion animals.

THE KITTENS AND THE PUPPIES are the ones who show him the way. The young ones direct him toward that which he seeks by their total trust, total inhibition and undiluted adoration of him. Had it not been for the kittens, whose lives he saved, and the puppies, who admired him at first sight, the puppies whose names are Emmett, Lolly, Snowball, Cotton, Silky and Day, who could've been Petal's clone but for his gender, the puppies whose names he learned because they were engraved on red hearts that dangled from brightly colored collars, had it not been for them he might have found himself stuck in a rut. Tiny's family whose names he knew because they, too, had thoughtful sturdy red shaped hearts. All of the dogs' names had obviously been bestowed with tenderness and consideration. Tenderness and consideration which had never been demonstrated to Tiny for the entirety of her life. He knew. He saw where she came from and he knows where she wound up, and that she wound up where she was because of where she came from.

Yes indeed, the old white woman certainly did a number on him. Because of her curse and the unfathomable pain that followed, Gerald becomes a human being. And to his surprise, he finds that though he's never felt so vulnerable, nor has he ever felt so alive. He's relieved that the transformation is taking place in front of eyes and minds that will never think him a fool, though he most assuredly is one of the greatest to ever walk the planet.

It's on the walks in the surrounding forest with the dogs that he deepens the breadth of the curse. The only ones he allows to come on the long walks are Harriet, Poof and Brownie. Ruger always stays behind with the puppies. Petal and Jasmine's bodies have been too sorely used and the long treks are difficult and worrisome for them. Harriet, Poof and Brownie are younger, and run down pine straw strewn trails with delight and strength. He feels their muscles and minds appreciating the exercise and sights. It has taken weeks for him to stop berating himself for making these incredible, intelligent creatures live their lives in their own filth and feces on six foot chains, and squalid accommodations. He will never do something so malign again.

He knows his physical healing is proceeding more rapidly than normal because of his routine. His daily routine of caring, being loved, nurturing others, and zero acts of violence. His feelings for the puppies are confusing. He doesn't understand them. They're intense while being completely innocent. He monitors their health while ensuring their safety. He makes sure their minds are stimulated and their bodies made strong.

He has laughed more than ever. Genuine laughter absent of any Machiavellian calculation. One day, he thinks, out of the blue, that if he had children, this is what he'd do for them. He's suddenly greatly saddened because if he would do this for his dogs, with purpose, planning, forethought and pleasure, surely a mother would want to do the same for a child she carried in her womb, to whom she gave birth, suckled at her breast, and never gave birth to another. Yet he feels no anger. Only sadness which the dogs chase away when they move toward him, sensing a need to share comfort. Gerald, the greatest fool to ever walk the earth, accepts their hugs and kisses, and no longer embarrassed to love, returns their affection fourfold.

The dogs have changed him. Dogs have turned him into a human being. He's lucid enough to realize that he's not the first person whose life has been completely transformed by companion animals. Book after book after book arrives and educates him on all things animal, but with a super charged focus on dogs and cats. Quentin, Quincey, Quantum and Qani fascinate him to no end. Their elegance and gentleness soothe his spirit. Their bravery among twelve Pitbulls bred for kill fighting astounds and amazes him. Animals are extraordinary.

He feels their curiosity, their consideration of their surroundings, their interest in their family, and he is humbled by the profound simplicity of their point of view. Humans need to take note of the civility to be witnessed in the gathering of animals. He observes how they get along, share, comfort, and even defend one another.

He looks out onto the green grass of the front lawn and what he sees is a family. It only took four abandoned kittens for the notion to finally penetrate his obstinate mind. A person's dogs and cats are his or her family. They bring layers of richness and growth to the family unit. And like children, teach one to be more compassionate, less selfish. The person who has animals and treats them as family members will inevitably have his or her world view spring wide open.

Petal, Jasmine, Harriet, Poof, Brownie, Ruger, Emmett, Snowball, Silky, Cotton, Lolly, Day and The Qat Quartet, Quentin, Quincey, Quantum and Qani. He speaks each name aloud and feels the love each and every one directs toward him, except Ruger. Ruger's suspicion has yet to fade. But this too only indicates a depth that he respects and is grateful to be aware of. He likes that when they look at him that he feels the forever of it. They will love and admire him forever. They will follow him wherever he leads. Except for Ruger, they trust him. They want him to always be near.

New Gerald smiles at them, winks at Ruger, and nods his head, knowing that they understand he respects them too. That the days of his ignorance are past, that finally what they feel is what he feels. The wonder of it is sanity in its purest form.

WHILE HE WAITS for Tiny to return he reads books on animal husbandry, carpentry, gardening, land management, and poultry farming. When he's bored he manages the vast financial empire he began building at age seven. Finance administration and multiplication of money is one of Gerald's gifts. He's not really interested in it. He doesn't care about being mega rich, though he's not far from it.

For Gerald, the building and manipulation of wealth is a hobby that barely engages one percent of his brain. He is his only competition, but no greater challenger could he have found. For two hours each day, five days a week, he checks his accounts and scours the world for undiscovered investment opportunities. He possesses the canny ability of uncovering criminal activity, which he'll follow for fun to exploit, or until he gets bored and outwits them because it's too easy. Sometimes he follows the trail to the source, and then methodically destroys the source once his bank account reflects the bounty from his precise exploitation.

Thus, Gerald becomes richer and richer as each day passes. Some people knit. Gerald outwits.

He has tried to locate Tiny by using the internet and multiple private investigators on the ground. But she continues to elude him. He can feel her stress, her fatigue, her hunger, her despondency and loneliness, her worry, and of late, her fear. He has not felt her fear this strongly and consistently. Something is nagging at her. Something is wrong and she feels powerless. But try as he might to figure out where she could be with the limited means she has, and no legitimate ID, he still hasn't even come close to finding her.

One night very late, he bolts up from the bed wide awake. He wakes up panting, as though he has been running full blast for a mile. He's getting out of the bed when he's thrown violently back onto it. He feels fists punch his stomach and hands slap his face so hard his ears ring. He feels the clothes ripped from her body, and then, he feels the rape and violation of Tiny in every unimaginable and imaginable way.

Whatever multiple young men consumed with thoughts of depraved and violent sex can do to a four foot nine inch tall woman who doesn't even weigh one hundred pounds, who was walking then frantically running home from a sixteen hour shift, who decided to take a short cut because she was so tired. Gerald feels everything. But because he's a changed man, he immediately recalls what he subjected Tiny to for so many years and because the old white woman's curse has no mercy in it, he feels every rape and every beating Tiny ever endured because of him. This night, Tiny suffers for forty-three minutes. Gerald writhes in unending agony, revulsion and self loathing until unconsciousness finally reprieves him.

The moment he regains consciousness he reaches for his phone so that he can put his vast resources to work. It isn't long before he feels a drug like sedation and he knows that Tiny is receiving professional medical care, somewhere. He knows that if he doesn't find her now, he may never do it. And with the deepest of sorrow and complete resignation, he realizes that when he finds her she will never voluntarily see him. That the feelings of the very thought of him, which the attack has reawakened, make her want to vomit and scream.

# Chapter 9

Darlene Cauley was let go from her teaching position three years ago. At the time, she had exactly one year remaining before she could enjoy full retirement benefits. The shock of it was emotionally traumatic. Her daughters urged her to take time off before heading back into the work force. They told her she'd been working since she was sixteen years old, that she could afford a year to reflect, relax and make a game plan. After a year of semi-blissful reprieve, much of which was spent on fuming about being let go, a lot of feeling sorry for herself, and then a good bit of resentment that none of her colleagues of the past twenty-nine years had called or dribbled by some job leads, the thing was, she was having substantial difficulty growing any interest in her skills and expertise.

At the end of the year she had no job, and no job prospects in sight. So far she'd been unable to find another teaching job or any job that paid a living wage. Apparently, educated, highly skilled fifty-six year old women were not sought after on the job market.

Two years later she's still unemployed, and in twenty-four hours she'll be homeless as well. All of her savings have been depleted. Yesterday, her house was formally repossessed by the bank. The legal writ is in the manila folder on top of her folding tv tray which stands next to the folding lawn chair, which is next to the single bed air mattress on the floor.

---

The estate sale of all of her worldly goods, which took place three months ago, only provided her with enough money to pay off her Toyota Highlander. Darlene paid off the car because she knew, if the worst happened, which surely it wouldn't, she'd need some place to live, and living in her paid for car was better than under a plastic tarp on some sidewalk. If it ever came to that, which no way in the world could she imagine it would, and so thought every homeless person on the planet.

She hasn't informed her daughters of her plight. Honestly, she was still a little in denial until the manila envelope arrived and she had to sign for it. It's definitely real. There was nothing fake about the uniformed officer who handed her the pen. And there's nothing fake about the date under her signature on the last page. Tomorrow her phone service will end. How can she get a job with no phone? How can she get a job when no one wants to hire her?

The phone rings and she stares at it. She doesn't want to talk to anyone. It rings. One more ring and it'll go to voice mail. She decides to answer it because she literally has nothing else to do. She manages to sound convincingly cheerful and well fed.

The call is from one of the six employment agencies in town that have her résumé. One of the six agencies where she has taken, and aced, reading tests, typing tests and workforce skills tests every three months for the past two years. This is the first call she has had from any of them. Why should they call her when she calls them every Monday at nine and every Friday at four thirty? For two years. A woman who sounds like she's nineteen years old informs her that a household management company would like to hire her, however, the job begins tomorrow morning at eight and is a live-in position. When the nineteen year old tells her the salary, Darlene is surprised how calm her voice sounds as she accepts the offer and requests the address. She does ask the teenager to repeat the salary, just to make sure she hasn't fantasized it.

The teenager tells her a copy of the terms are being sent to her email as they speak. She instructs her that she'll need her signature before she can formally accept the offer on her behalf. Darlene thanks the teenager, hangs up, then opens her email on the phone whose contract ends tomorrow.

She signs it without reading it, waits five minutes then sends it back to the employment agency. While the signed work agreement is racing back to the agency, Darlene lies down on the air mattress and stares at the salary she'll receive. She finds herself shaking from fear, then relief, then fear laced with relief. The amount of money she'll be paid is almost triple that of her yearly salary as a teacher. And she'll have a place to live as well? It sounds too good to be true. What if her new boss is a drug lord? But what would a drug lord need from a fifty-six year old high school teacher?

She begins packing her clothes immediately. Tomorrow she'll fold up the tv tray and lawn chair, deflate the mattress and leave them in the garage for the bank. Once her suitcase is packed she decides to go to the library and print out the contract. There's also an attachment in the email she hasn't looked at.

After she downloads the attachment and prints it, she discovers that what she had signed was the agency contract, not her new employer's contract. When she has the document in hand and is seated in a proper chair in front of a proper table she learns there are financial contingencies. There's always a catch. But there's also good news – she was born for this job.

She wouldn't realize the full salary amount or be awarded quarterly bonuses unless the client agrees to receive all education. If the client agrees to learn, then the bonuses would arrive only if certain grades are achieved. The higher the grades, the bigger the rewards, the longer the term of the agreement. In sum, as long as the client learned, Darlene had a job.

Darlene Cauley, newly employed, leaves the library and drives home. She does not eat because she can't afford to. On the way home she reflects on her years as an educator. She was top rated in the state every single year. She received Teacher of the Year on six separate occasions, even the year before she was released, let go, fired. Her teaching skills were knowledgeable, enthusiastic and superb. More than anything, she loved to teach, to educate.

When she arrives home she walks to the empty master suite and into the master closet. On the right side behind the door is another door. She opens it, turns on the light, closes the door and then screams at the top of her lungs. She sings songs and dances. She whoops and yells with joy until her throat hurts. She laughs hysterically because there's nowhere else for this episode to go.

Finally, spent and exhausted, she falls to her knees and thanks God, then she thanks her dearly departed husband Don for constructing the twelve by twelve sound proof panic room, which had remained unused until now. There'd never been a call to panic. Perhaps, from now on, she'd call it the Unbridled Joy Room.

Darlene has coffee for breakfast, and nothing else. She received a text from her employer at seven that morning. The employment contract stipulated that all employer/employee communication would be via texting. This would be the first and last text she would receive on her personal phone. Her business phone would arrive before noon today, along with other deliveries. A large delivery will arrive at one o'clock. Her client would arrive at four. The text instructs her where the key to the home is located.

Two longer texts inform her she will be responsible for the upkeep and maintenance of the house and grounds. If her duties to the client interfere with these tasks, she is to inform her employer immediately so that additional personnel can be hired. Her client's education is to assume top priority. She's to consult with her client to determine exactly which implements and equipment will be required to maintain order of the premises and grounds if what has been provided is inadequate.

Darlene receives this last text just as she's pulling out of the driveway of the home where she raised two beautiful daughters and loved a good husband. She looks back at the house she took care of, at the lawn she mowed, at flower beds she designed then filled with a mix of flowers and vegetables. She thinks the bank will have no trouble at all selling this charming, well cared for property.

She leaves without regret. A new chapter is beginning. She's nervous and excited. Who on earth has ever heard of a job like this?

When she pulls into the shaded driveway of mid century modern architectural masterpiece, she looks down at her phone to confirm the address. Houses in this famous neighborhood rarely come on the market. And when they do, no obtrusive for sale sign mars the beautifully landscaped lawns. They quietly pass from one owner to another, as there's a long list of individuals and families hankering to get into this subdivision. The location has always been wonderful, but with the resurgence of the just far enough away downtown area, living in this neighborhood has become especially sought after, and coveted by many. Though not all can afford the price tags.

Each home is a custom designed architectural gem. There are no vacancies. No boarded windows, no unkempt yards, no leaking roofs, no missing shingles, no trees touching roofs. The gardens are mature, well monitored and trained. Where in this day and age could one see so many healthy mature camellias, live oaks, massive towering magnolias allowed to grow as they will, and all those ivy covered fences?

The people who are fortunate enough to live into this neighborhood realize they're fortunate. They appreciate, value and take care of their properties. They nurture life in all its forms. On her drive through the neighborhood, Darlene sees neighbors speaking to one another, people jogging, pushing strollers, trimming hedges, birds and squirrels feeding from feeders, cats lounging on cushioned chairs on front porches, and best of all, dogs lying on green grass in the sun, dogs walking on leashes, dogs jogging beside their owners, dogs watching their masters plant plants, and dogs playing with small children and other dogs.

So Darlene is to be the housekeeper, cook, gardener, chauffeur and educator. Her job is to do everything she loves. And for what she's being paid, she would've gladly been the pedicurist as well. Lack and suffering will surely turn a mind to gratitude and wonder, she muses.

She'd never been in one of these homes, but like everyone else in the city, she'd always wanted to. The extra large door is painted high gloss turquoise blue and the shining heavy brass door knob is in the exact middle. There's only one window on the front of the house. It's a long rectangle to the right of the front door, between the front door and the double garage door.

There are scads of boxes and packages that block her path for ten feet. The majority are from online pet stores. She feels her heart begin to pound in hope and excitement. Her fourteen year old Pit Bull mix, Sasha Lynn, had passed away shortly after Darlene had lost her job. The dog had been a cherished family member since she was adopted from the local high kill shelter at twelve weeks of age. She missed her terribly. Sasha Lynn had been adopted two weeks after the death of her husband. She doesn't know what she would've done without that beautiful girl. Sasha Lynn pulled her from her grief, kept her fit, kept her company, kept her smiling, and best of all, made her spirit thrive. She'd not gotten another pet after her passing because her financial circumstances prohibited it.

As she makes her way to the front door, she picks up boxes of all sizes and weight. This person must have a lot of dogs. Then her heart dips a little and she fears her client may be mentally ill, a hoarder, one of those weirdos who mistakes dogs for children and people. There are so many boxes. She pauses to listen. She hears no dogs.

She inserts the key into the knob and turns it. The lock clicks and the solid wood door opens wide on well oiled hinges. Darlene gasps. The entire back wall is glass. And it's not the glass that was initially installed. This is high tech modern glass and it is stunning. The interior walls are all white. The floors are flawless terrazzo and shine like new. There's a narrow wood table against the left foyer wall. She places her bag and the key on it. First order of business is to explore this beauty!

The small foyer opens onto a large living room that has sleek low red leather sofas placed to a stylish advantage. There are wooden end tables, but no coffee tables. There's a large fireplace on the right wall. The wall surrounding it is an unusual green stone and complements the terrazzo perfectly.

She looks out of the eight foot tall picture windows onto a perfect yard that must be an acre long and  two acres wide. There's a large swimming pool with two live oaks on either side of it but far enough away so the leaves won't overwhelm it in the fall. There are chairs and tables underneath one of the trees. There's a gargantuan magnolia that is twenty feet away from the left back roof of the fourteen foot deep covered patio that runs along the entirety of the rear of the home.

Darlene goes left and discovers  a minimalist but sumptuous master suite that comprises a small office, a small den, a large bedroom, and a  gorgeous master bath. There's a soaking tub that abuts the glass wall so that the bather can bask in soothing water while enjoying all the sights and sounds of nature. She sees that the wall of glass can be opened completely, giving the bather the illusion of bathing outdoors. It's too lovely and considered for words.

The king size bed has no bedding on it. Darlene begins opening cabinets that reveal themselves to be empty. She's about to continue her exploration when the doorbell rings. When she walks back into the living room she sees a flat screen tv on the wall across from the back picture windows has an image on it. The UPS man is neatly uniformed and waiting for her.

He has boxes and packages from a food delivery company. As he drives away, the local grocery delivery van pulls into the semi circle drive. She directs the driver and his loaded dolly through the living room toward a doorway she hopes will lead to the kitchen.

It is indeed the kitchen, and as they enter both stop in their tracks to stand and gawk at the modern magnificence of a kitchen that any cook, or chef, would give their eyeteeth to get their hands on and into.

The countertops are continuous slabs of calacatta marble and must have cost a fortune because there are yards and yards of it. Even the backsplashes are slab calacatta marble. The appliances are commercial grade and shine with their brand spanking newness. The cabinets are dove gray and bring out a different beauty in the terrazzo floors. No doubt about it, this room is the showpiece of this incredible home.

While Darlene continues to gawk at the utilitarian extravagance, the grocery delivery man puts his boxes on the countertop, then leaves for more. Darlene barely notices his coming and going as she opens the ovens, looks at the six eyes on the gas range, with a griddle between them, inspects the wood burning pizza oven, opens the convection microwave, turns on one of the two faucets on the six foot long stainless steel sink, pulls out drawers filled with recently purchased flatware, pots and pans of all manner, white china dishes, sparkling clear glassware and finally, every size of every roll of foil paper, plastic wrap and Ziploc bag any human cook or chef will ever need.

She notices a white folded card on the vast marble covered island and opens it. It's a thank you note from a kitchen consulting group expressing gratitude for using their services, and politely asking to not hesitate to call them at any time for any further culinary equipment needs. The card has yesterday's date on it.

She returns the thank you note to the countertop when the grocery delivery man gains her attention to say good bye. She looks up to thank him as well and discovers that half of the island countertop is loaded with double stacked boxes of groceries. She shakes herself out of her reverie, accompanies the delivery man to the door, and as he leaves she begins bringing the boxes in front of the front door into the house. She has a lot of work to do. The text was clear that the home must be in order by four o'clock. If she manages it, she gets a five hundred dollar signing bonus.

Once all of the boxes are inside she returns to the kitchen to unload the groceries. There's a pantry that's the size of her former bedroom. There's a laundry room that's twice the size of the pantry. There are two large freezers, another refrigerator, two washers, two dryers, a folding station and a wall of nothing but floor to ceiling storage consisting of shelved storage closets and deep drawers. On the opposite wall, next to the door leading to a full bath with shower is a professional grade dog washing station replete with stainless steel tubs and a grooming table. Does her client show dogs? But needs an education? Does her employer know she was just a high school teacher?

She can't worry. She will not worry. She will not doubt. If she gets the house in order by four o'clock, a five hundred dollar bonus will be sent to her bank account today, which after the morning coffee splurge, holds four dollars and seventy six cents. To work she goes!

The first box she opens has two top of the line cell phones in it. There are also two clips so that she can have it with her always. She plugs them in to discover they're fully charged. One has a text, so it must be hers. She's informed the main delivery will arrive thirty minutes after her client's arrival. The extra time is a relief. She clips the phone to her waistband and begins unpacking.

The majority of the boxes of groceries are ten pound bags of leg quarters. She's astonished by the amount of leg quarters. But her astonishment is slowing her down so she stops giving into gawking bewilderment and begins organizing. All but two bags of the leg quarters go into one of the laundry room freezers. One

---

freezer is now full of nothing but leg quarters. She organizes with efficiency the many cans of vegetables, jars of spaghetti sauce, bottles of ketchup and salad dressings, bags of rice and noodles, loaves of nutritious bread, bags of frozen vegetables, every type of spice she has ever seen and then many she's never heard of, bags of flour and sugar, bags of coffee, thousands of coffee filters, sliced meat, bacon, steaks, fish, ground beef, ribs, and a two foot tall stack of frozen gourmet pizzas minus one, which she leaves out and pops into the oven for herself.

While the pizza bakes she quickly breaks down the boxes until they're flat, then she heads into the living room to continue unpacking. She unpacks dog toys, dog chews, cushioned dog pads, ten bags of dog food, dog collars, dog shampoo, dog grooming equipment, flea and tick prevention, seven large elevated dog beds she must assemble. But where are the dogs? The large dogs, apparently. This house has no dog smell in it.

She opens boxes filled with water proof mattress pads, at least twenty bedspreads, ten sets of king size Egyptian cotton linens, a huge assortment of towels, bath mats, soap, shampoo, razors, shaving cream, essential oils, powder, heating pads, fragrance and diffusers.

There are scissors, sponges, brushes, household cleaning products, huge bags of washer and dishwasher detergent pods. Enough first aid ointment, sprays, lotions and bandaging materials to meet any minor or near major emergency.

She takes the sheets and towels to the laundry room and is grateful for two washers. She thinks she'll have her client's bed made and room sorted in plenty of time. As she turns on the second wash, the oven and doorbell ding simultaneously. She removes her perfectly cooked pizza from the oven and goes to the front door.

While Darlene eats a delicious slice of gourmet frozen pizza she could never bring herself to buy, she watches the water delivery man set up a water dispenser and then haul in ten five gallon replacements. He asks her if she needs a paper cup dispenser. She tells him no, and then with unconcealed delight shows him the two dishwashers on either side of the six foot kitchen sink.

She's walking toward the back yard for an up close viewing of the pool when her new phone trills like a bird. She has a text.

# Chapter 10

From secret cameras installed throughout the home, Gerald watches Darlene Cauley work and organize like a house on fire. He's in the living room sitting on the sofa. The Lady Team, Ruger and Emmett are outside. Which is odd. It's as if they know something is up. His Crew -- Snowball, Cotton, Silky, Lolly, Day and The Qat Quartet are with him. The Qat Quartet are still in the shoebox. They're on Gerald's lap with the heating pad on his thighs. The puppies are asleep on the floor, elevated beds and on whichever piece of furniture they wish to be on.

Through his network of private investigators, paid informants and sundry individuals he's been paying to find Tiny, he knew after the attack he'd at last be able to locate her. She'd be taken to a hospital. Because he had felt the attack abruptly stop, right in the middle of blows and penetration. It just stopped. This meant that other people had come upon the scene and been seen by the attackers, causing the attackers to flee.

When he regained consciousness he made calls, sent texts and emails to people he had hired to find her. Within an hour he knew which hospital she had been taken to, the extent of her injuries and her room number. The pain in his lower region prevented him from sitting up so he'd dragged his laptop onto the bed and hacked into the hospital records. He learned what each injury cost to treat. Next, he established an account for her and deposited enough money to cover all of her expenses.

Gerald is in a great deal of physical pain, and though he won't realize it, or admit it, until years later, he's in a great deal of spiritual pain, too. He has pushed back the main delivery arrival time. He has pushed back the main delivery time because he wants to see Tiny. Even as he knows that she doesn't want to see him or be anywhere near him, he wants to see her because he knows she'll be completely unaware of his presence. He thinks his physical pain is causing all of his current discomfort. It's not. It's only causing fifty percent of it

The leaden weight he feels on his shoulders, his chest and legs is not the resulting aftermath of an intense physical assault. It's the beginning of a heartbreak he doesn't believe is possible, but he has a vague, a very vague suspicion that some of the hurt he's feeling is from what he's about to do. He will take The Lady Team, Ruger and Emmett to Tiny. His Crew and The Qat Quartet will remain with him.

When he took Tiny's suitcase filled with used dog toys to the old beat up SUV he'd forced her to drive, he looked around and saw that the Lady Team, Ruger and Emmett did not follow him back inside. That was at ten thirty. It's now two o'clock and they're still waiting by the vehicle. It's as if they know they're going to her, their sister. Savior of Emmett. Grand love of Ruger's life.

The heavy insistent weight he feels is sorrow. As he watches the exceedingly well chosen Darlene dart around the house unpacking, organizing and looking around in wonder, he eventually admits to himself that his feelings are hurt. He did not expect The Lady Team to want to abandon him so easily. Especially Petal, whom he favors the most. He is especially saddened by her eager defection, and to his confusion, admits he will miss her terribly. He, Gerald The Despicable, is on the verge of tears because a dog is leaving his life.

He checks on The Qat Quartet once more then resumes watching the industrious actions of Darlene. He has decided he'll pay her the five hundred dollar bonus whether or not she gets everything done on time. It'll be close enough.

When he realized that Tiny would never willingly come back to him, he began making plans to help her. He'd find a way to help her whether she wanted his help or not. He knew he had to do it in such a manner that she couldn't say no, that to say no to him would ruin the life of another. That's when he found Darlene's profile on the employment agency website. When he hacked her employment records at the school board and her bank accounts, he knew she was in fact, already ruined, but her ruin made her the perfect person for the job. He was on the verge of assuming her derelict loan when everything changed in a horrible way, and it turned out that Darlene's encroaching homelessness worked wonderfully to his advantage.

She doesn't look like the employment photo taken two and half years ago. She's much thinner, haggard, and desperately needs a dye job. Despite that, this is a good woman of strong character who had been done wrong by the indifferent bureaucracy of the school system. Old Gerald thinks so what, that's the way things roll. Nobody cares because nobody cares. New Gerald watches her taking fresh smelling linens from the dryer, making the bed of a stranger to perfection. Fluffing down filled pillows, tucking here, tucking there until the bed is a housekeeping masterpiece. New Gerald thinks that she hasn't even looked for her room or been concerned about her comfort. He knows the bonus is needed but not what drives her. Into his life has come the second most selfless person he's ever known.

Gerald has owned the home for five years. Over the years he upgraded whenever the meanness struck him. When this home was featured one afternoon on a television program and Tiny mentioned how beautiful she thought it was, the next day he moved them into a dilapidated two bedroom mobile home. He didn't tell her he'd purchased the beautiful home that evening.

And so it went. Whenever Tiny mentioned the way a room looked, the style and fabric of a piece of furniture, a flooring type she appreciated, or a bathroom she found pretty, Gerald would do his best to provide her with the exact opposite while reconfiguring and installing her choices in this house, for spite.

Chic low slung red leather sofas became smelly used couches covered in miserable fabric that one felt velcroed to immediately upon sitting down. The struggle to extricate oneself from the depths of the couches was real. Gerald always had a pleather recliner no one was to use but him.

One day Tiny mentioned she didn't like carpet so every room she lived in became wall to wall carpet, even the bathroom she used, even the laundry room she needed. His areas were always unattractive ceramic tile, that may or may not have been the same color and shape. He kept the ugliness factor very high. It wasn't difficult, considering how ugly he was on the inside.

As he watches Darlene take great care in every task she undertakes he begins noticing the renovation results, and he thinks what excellent taste Tiny has. When he gave orders for the remodeling he didn't think or take time to consider color schemes, appliance brands and types, or room sizes, or bathroom layouts. He simply told the renovators to do what he'd heard Tiny say she liked. Every mention she ever made of anything having to do with having a house a certain way, he made sure it happened in this house while making sure the exact opposite occurred in the home she inhabited.

He'd been working on this house for five years. Everything had been updated. To all practical purposes, this home, dreamed up and then constructed in1945, was brand new. He hadn't made up his mind what to do with the house. But certainly it would've involved hurting Tiny's feelings, and the never ending work of crushing her spirit.

The curse of the old white woman made him forget about the house. He had completely forgotten about it. He never cared about it anyway. He'd bought and remodeled it to be mean. To continue his unrelenting tormenting reign over Tiny. He had been trying to crush Tiny's spirit for almost a decade and had been unsuccessful. The only thing he knew for sure he'd accomplished was making her life miserable. Her spirit would not be crushed. No matter what undesirable task he forced her to do. She would not be broken. Depressed, yes, despondent, no. How could she be despondent when she had so much love and kindness in her life every single day? Never from a human. But from five female Pit Bulls he always had imprisoned and enslaved in the back yard. Whatever violence he perpetrated on her was soon assuaged with responsive gentleness and soul healing friendship. He gets it now.

He spends most of his days with The Lady Team. They go with him on walks and rides in the golf cart. He feels a deeper connection with them than with His Crew. Perhaps because he has sought to have a deeper connection. He talks to them, pets them, plays with them and watches them as they interact. It's fascinating, and if he knew how much they needed to touch and be touched by one another, how well they got a long, he would've... Done absolutely nothing. Maybe he would've even had sound proof concrete walls built between them to totally isolate them from all connection to life. He's so glad he didn't know.

Maybe it's shame that motivates him to spend so much time with The Lady Team. He doesn't know. He's not to the point where he can or wants to figure that out. He only knows that when he's with them he feels better, all over. His mind is calmer, his heart beats slower, his muscles relax, he's more aware of life. His sadistic tendencies are cured by the revelation of their uniqueness, their depth of intelligence and the empathy for those who enter their orbit. Will His Crew be the same? He'll soon know the answer to that because in one hour he leaves to leave them. When he feels his throat constrict he looks down to check on The Qat Quartet. They're tiny, but they're alive. And by reaching for the feeding syringes on the end table, he'll make sure they stay that way.

DARLENE RECEIVES A TEXT with a recipe for "Dog Stew". That's what it says, "Dog Stew Recipe". She is to make sure double quantity recipes are prepared and ready by two o'clock tomorrow. She's headed toward the kitchen to prep when the doorbell rings.

As she signs for the three huge boxes she asks the delivery man if he wouldn't mind bringing them into the foyer as they appear to be very heavy. He uses his dolly to fulfill her request. Darlene closes the door, and as she does is pleased to note that all of the boxes which were ten feet deep to the front door have been unpacked, the items put away or put together. The boxes have been flattened and are waiting curbside for the trash pickup tomorrow.

She retrieves a brand new knife from a kitchen drawer and quickly cuts the tape away from all three boxes. Though none of the items and goods are for her, it has felt like Christmas today. It has been a true pleasure to unpack and organize, or assemble, these beautifully made things. Even the cleaning supplies were the best on the market. Their bright festive labels beam like a cheerful rainbow when she opens various cabinet doors.

As she pulls back brown packing paper, then crinkly white tissue paper, she's delighted to see what is revealed. Women's clothing! So her client is a woman. But a very little woman if she's to interpret anything from the size of the garments she unfolds. Before she continues she retrieves two armfuls of hangers from her client's empty closet.

Shirts and pants of different styles and fabric fill one box. Two down coats, one fire engine red, one bright orange, soft sweaters of cashmere and wool blends fill another. Sweatshirts, yoga pants, t shirts, underwear, pajamas, nightgowns and four pairs of expensive athletic shoes fill the last. She spies a lovely thin burled wood box on the bottom as she removes the last box of shoes. She's on the verge of opening it when the doorbell rings yet again. Her phone trills as well and when she looks at it she's informed the last delivery is on schedule. It's four o'clock on the dot. She quickly breaks down the last box and places the wood box on the foyer table before she opens the door with a smile on her face.

Her smile disappears as she views a tiny unconscious woman on an ambulance gurney. Two uniformed paramedics wheel the portable bed into the house and follow Darlene to the master suite. She supervises as the man carefully and slowly lifts her up and places her on the bed. Darlene moves in quickly to situate the pillow and to pull the white cotton bedding to her chest. As she shoos the paramedics from the room she closes all of the curtains with a flick of a switch.

Darlene feels protective of this lady. She doesn't know her, but all day long she has unpacked and organized things that were evidently chosen with great care and attention. Thus, she mistakenly assumes this invalid woman is beloved and cherished. She hopes and prays she's wonderful instead of spoiled.

Jill, the female paramedic, hands her the requisite paperwork as she leaves. Darlene is closing the front door when she sees an old beat up SUV pull into the driveway. She's about to walk out to meet it when the garage door opens and the SUV pulls forward, then backs right in. She closes the door, props the last flattened box against the left foyer wall and walks quickly through the kitchen toward the door to the garage. She's placing the paperwork the paramedic gave her on the kitchen island when the door opens and a massive, overmuscled, white dog bounds through it and runs toward her client's bedroom. Alarmed, Darlene races after him.

Gerald watches Darlene run after Ruger. He's not worried. He knows Ruger won't harm Tiny because he's so acutely aware of her, yet desperate to be near her again, to smell her. He keeps Emmett on a leash. He thinks Ruger would kill him if he jumped on the bed in excitement. He watches The Lady Team trot toward the back bedroom with heads held high, bodies and tails wagging happily back and forth. Poof passes gas as she walks from the kitchen into the living room. He's pretty sure she'll do so again shortly.

Gerald looks around the kitchen and sees that Darlene has taken fresh cuttings from the yard and placed them in water in a large vase in the middle of the island. The paramedic papers lay nearby at an angle. There's no need for him to look at them as he knows every detail of them.

He notices how dark Tiny's room is. Darlene must have closed the curtains all of the way. The bedroom curtains are lined with blackout fabric. He sends a text to Darlene.

Darlene is panting and standing beside a motionless Tiny when her phone trills. The huge white dog had run into the room and right up to the bed. Darlene was so afraid he was about to jump onto the bed, but she watched in wonder as he simply smelled the length of her client's slim form, head to toe, twice, then gently licked her immobile hand. After his inspection and confirmation, he'd padded around to the other side of the bed, and with the grace and silence of a cat, had leapt onto it without disturbing anything. Stupefied, she watched as he gently positioned himself next to her client until his back was lined up parallel to her side. There was no doubt in her mind that this dog weighed more than twice that of the woman he was lying next to. And she'd swear on a Bible he'd immediately fallen asleep. Before she reads the text, Darlene thinks he's much too skinny.

The text informs her that her client has a fear of the dark and is never to be left alone without a light on, no matter if the dogs are with her or not. A light is to be left on in every room of the home, including bathrooms, always. Darlene turns and walks into the bathroom where she turns on a light and leaves the door open.

When she comes back into the bedroom there's a sight to behold. Five female Pit Bulls are standing alongside the bed. All of their chins are perched along the edge as they gaze in adoration at the face of the sleeping woman. Darlene smiles in relief and awe to see such a dear sight. Their tails are moving slowly back and forth. It's as though they know their master, because these dogs belong to this woman, who lies silently in an injured, vulnerable and fragile state. Suddenly she smells something officious, like a dead animal.

"It's Poof," says Gerald, the pretend delivery man. "She passes gas whenever she's happy and surrounded by her family. She's the blue brindle. The one in the middle. You've got a lot of mail in your mailbox. I'll wait here until you get back. This is Emmett. You can take him with you if you like. He may not understand why he can't jump on the bed. And if he does, Ruger might hurt him. You'll need to be careful and patient until he understands. He's just a puppy," Gerald says as he hands her the leash.

Darlene takes the leash from him. She can't make out his features because he's standing in a darkened area of the bedroom but she gladly accepts the assistance. She doesn't want to be far from her client for long. She and Emmett leave to get the mail.

Gerald moves toward the bed when Darlene leaves the room. He turns on the bedside table light and the soft glow washes over Tiny's face. He looks down at her. The Lady Team moves away when he comes near. Petal and Jasmine jump onto the bed while Poof, Brownie and Harriet lie down next to it.

Tiny's face looks as it always has, except now he notices the graceful contours he purposefully ignored. Her high cheekbones, her smooth skin, a brow that boasts too many worry lines. Eyes with long eyelashes and too few laughter lines. Why hadn't he seen what a pretty woman she'd become?

He remembers the day he met her. Even then she looked like a child. He remembers her turning around to him in class on that first day, her shy but welcoming smile. She was the only one at school who was nice to him. He remembers her repeated acts of generosity and friendship. She'd never been anything but kind to him.

He wants to apologize. To convince her he's sorry and ashamed of everything. He'd give everything he possesses to have Tiny completely healed, yet have her remain forever suffering with comprehensive incurable amnesia.

He hears the front door shut, the click of Emmett's nails. He quickly wipes his eyes and cheeks. Is this the last time he'll be with her? He looks at Ruger and knows it won't be long before he gains his weight back. He looks at The Lady Crew.

Petal and Jasmine look at him then lower their heads to the bed to sleep. Poof, Brownie and Harriet look at him as if to say, "Ok, we're good. See you around. Bye." He feels how relaxed they are. He feels the full physical and mental relief of Ruger. He hadn't realized how tense he'd been until now. He can see his dreams. They're dreams of Tiny. Nothing of him. No thought of him. It's as though he has already been completely forgotten.

He can feel Emmett bonding with Darlene. He feels the drugged curative sleep of Tiny. He feels his heart pounding in his chest so hard and fast he thinks he's going to have a stroke. But he knows he's not. That there's more suffering in store for him. Some of it happening this instant, with these dogs he erroneously assumed would miss him. They won't miss him at all. The hours that were spent together was a gift from them to him that he didn't deserve. He's learning that about dogs. They're givers, not takers. They share; they don't hoard.

In the all too brief time he has spent and gotten to know The Lady Team, he has learned more about his deficiencies than ever. He can't think of any deficiencies a dog has. He knows The Lady Team is precious and wonderful because of the manner in which Tiny treated them. Even when she was not present, he benefitted from her generosity and love. The dogs taught him that. He hopes he can continue her legacy with His Crew and The Qat Quartet. He'll surely try.

He gazes once more at the pretty peaceful shape of Tiny's face. He studies every curve and nuance in appreciation and respect. Once satisfied, he looks at the huge sleeping shape of Ruger and whispers,

"You better watch out for her, Ruger. All of you. And, and... I thank you for the generosity of your patience with me. I'll never forget it."

Darlene is crossing the foyer when the delivery man exits her client's bedroom. When she sees him, she stops in her tracks. Standing before her, young, lean, tall, lithe and muscular, is the most beautiful human being she has ever seen in her life. He's absolutely stunning, and she cannot stop staring. She thinks her mouth may be open as he walks past her without a word and leaves. She's still standing there gaping at nothing when she hears him drive away.

What an incredible day!

# Chapter 11

When Tiny awakens from her sedative induced sleep she thinks she's dreaming. The second before she opens her eyes, Ruger opened his. He raises his head to look at her. Tiny sees Ruger and isn't sure if it's actually him. The bones on his head are starkly visible and when she moves her hand over him she can feel his ribs. She looks around in lethargic slow motion, her mind cloudy and uncertain.

In the low light from the lamp next to her bed, she sees the closed floor to ceiling curtains. She sees Petal and Jasmine curled up and sleeping next to her feet on a huge bed. She sees Brownie and Poof on the floor, and Harriet in a nearby wingback chair. She thinks she's dreaming, and she loves this dream. She needs this dream. She makes no abrupt movement. She closes her eyes, feels a too thin Ruger settle back next to her, his warm body lined up perfectly to hers. She hears him sigh deeply. In the middle of caressing his food deprived body, she falls asleep.

Ruger lifts his head to stare at her. He looks at her chin, her cheeks, her brow and her closed eyes. He turns his head right and sees Emmett and the white lady standing in the doorway to the bedroom. He watches as the white lady takes in the scene, sees her smile, and watches her unlatch the leash from Emmett's collar. He attentively follows the progress of Emmett as he pads over to the bed to smell Tiny. His eyes don't leave Ruger and Ruger's eyes don't leave his. Once his nose has confirmed the identity of this protected and important human, he returns to Darlene's side. After all, Emmett has known only kindness and company since the day he was born. He adores Tiny, but he's young and wants to be where the action is.

As Tiny sleeps, dreaming the most marvelous dreams of her family and a peace filled inseparable existence, Darlene, standing in the doorway, takes in the quiet scene. She counts six Pit Bulls. She heard the extraordinary looking delivery man call the white one, Ruger. He doesn't look like any Pit Bull she's ever seen. She's never seen one built like him, with so many muscles. Plus the size of him. He's almost as tall as a Bull Mastiff. From where she stands she can see the clear outline of every one of his ribs and his hip bones. This reminds her to prepare the dog stew. Before turning off the bedside lamp, she plugs in night lights in all of the rooms of her client's suite, including the closet.

She and Emmett walk back to the kitchen after plugging in night lights in the living room, foyer and foyer closet. She plugs in two more in the kitchen, two in the laundry and one in the laundry bathroom. She has four remaining when it dawns on her she doesn't know where her bedroom is.

There's a closed louvered door next to the loveseat in the keeping room. It must lead to other bedrooms and the servant quarters. She takes her suitcase from the living room and walks through the door. It opens onto a six foot wide twenty foot long hall that has floor to ceiling windows on one side. There are hostas blooming in the flower bed beside the window. She sees so many different varieties of hostas and ferns. Two mature lace leaf maples grace either side of the flower bed. So much thought of the beautiful went into the planning of this home, both inside and out. She finds herself continually comforted by each new sight she comes upon.

She discovers there's only one other bedroom in the home, and it's an exact mirror of the master suite. She can't believe she'll have such a lovely private space to live in. All to herself. It's so glamourous. The bathroom looks like something out of a fancy architecture magazine.

She unpacks her clothes, places her paltry toiletries on the white marble bathroom countertop then quickly makes the bed with clean, fresh smelling, brand new luxurious cotton linens. Once finished with both the task and the admiration of the welcoming sight, she and Emmett stand at the foot of her king size bed and look out at the lawn. Spotting a mystery, she moves closer to windows.

"You know what, Emmett, I heard there was a property in this neighborhood with ten acres attached to it. And I'll bet you two treats that this is that very property. Look at that opening in the fence over there. You see it? Where does it go? Let's go explore, shall we? But first, let's see if broke Aunt Darlene has five hundred more dollars in her bank account."

Emmett sits on his haunches, looking up at her while she moves her index finger around on a small flat black rectangle. When she grins down at him as she puts the rectangle back on her hip, he opens his wide Pit Bull mouth to grin up at her, too. He loves this human already!

Darlene slides open the eight foot tall sliding glass door in her bedroom and it moves back as if of its own volition. It makes no noise as it glides to a stop, and she knows it must weigh a ton. She thinks whoever designed and built this house took not only great pride in his or her work, but impressing the client was a top priority.

"Mission accomplished, Emmett. Have you ever seen a house like this? Me either! Much less have the privilege of living in it full time. It's flawless, yet so warm and welcoming. We're going to make it a wonderful home. You'll be happy here, I just know it. And you know what, I have a feeling I will be, too."

Emmett and Darlene walk across a thick cushion of well tended St. Augustine grass toward the opening in the fence line, and sure enough, what must be the remaining acreage of the ten opens expansively before them. Emmett spies two squirrels and races across the field. Darlene sees a maintained pecan orchard of at least fifty trees. She sees fruit trees and fruit producing bushes, a large and attractive fenced area with at least ten raised beds full of nothing but rich looking soil. Her heart lifts in her chest. Her client gardens, too!

There are two long sheds behind the raised garden area. Between the sheds is an open area. As she walks closer she can see that there's chicken wire on both sides and the top. She's almost there when Emmett runs close to the wire and begins barking like a maniac. She allows him to continue because she has had surprise after surprise today and for all she knows, her client has crocodiles. But a crocodile does not waddle out or scurry toward the farthest corner. She counts thirty little fuzzy yellow and white chicks darting here and there, and finally, Emmett ceases his enthusiastic barking to stare in fascination. A chicken coop!

The glamour of the property begins to fade a little when she realizes how much work will be required to maintain it. She begins to understand the exorbitant pay she's to receive.

"Emmett, I've got my work cut out for me here. I hope I don't have a heart attack trying to do it all. But there's no choice. I've got to do it. This is what has been handed to me. It could be worse. I could be living in my car right now. Instead, I've got a new dog pal, no bills, food a plenty, and maybe a job that will be wonderful. Let's go see how your MamaLady's doing."

When Darlene walks away, Emmett stares longingly at the chicks for five seconds before trotting after her. When she starts jogging he thinks she wants to play and he takes off running full blast toward her. He runs circles around her until she starts laughing. Then he rolls on the grass and grins at the sky. He's so happy to be alive.

While Dog Stew simmers on the stove and Emmett chews on a juicy bone at her feet, Darlene eats gourmet pizza and reads the medical report on Emmaline Carruthers, the name of her client. It doesn't take a healthcare professional to understand the terrible and unspeakable injuries she sustained and endured. She was savagely raped and severely beaten on her chest, stomach and back. She has three broken ribs. Yet her prognosis is good if she receives proper care and adequate rest. The attending physician anticipates total healing for Miss Emmaline if the listed guidelines and recovery schedule are diligently adhered to. He has scrawled the name and phone number of a family therapist at the bottom of the last page.

Darlene places the papers back into the manila folder and wishes she could burn them. What sick individual or individuals would attack a woman that small? Cowards. A bunch of lily livered cowards. Perverts. Individuals with twisted minds. They're the ones who need the therapy! If Darlene knew how to cuss and swear she would do it with such gusto and sincerity right now it'd burn the ears off of a statue. It makes her so mad the way people treat other people. Her hands are shaking when she returns the folder to the countertop.

She feels Emmett lick her hand, then position his head underneath her hand so that it's on the top of his head and she need only make the barest of movements to pet him. She'll be comforted by him. She looks down at Emmett looking up at her. He has the blocky head of the Pit Bull but his body resembles that of the big white dog on Miss Emmaline's bed. He must be his offspring. Darlene squats down to hug Emmett and share her thoughts,

"Emmett, we need to be more like dogs. Why can't we get along like the animals? Do you ever hear of them attacking, killing or harming one another for no reason? We do it nonstop. We're continually hurting one another. Giving into rage, to sick, selfish, disgraceful desires. We steal from one another. Take things and people we don't need. We're so confused. Why can't we get along like animals? Cohabitating in peace. Sharing. Accepting hardship as part of a life that helps grow character and bring us closer together. Why must we always hurt one another? It makes no sense."

Emmett listens patiently to the new human. She smells interesting and he has always enjoyed hugs. Especially when they're real. He can tell when they're real, when the person means it. This human means it. His head is tucked against her ear and neck. He likes listening to her talk to him. He doesn't understand every word but he understands the tone of her voice. It has the sound of someone trying to figure something out and not being able to do it. He decides to lick her ear to let her know he's here for her. He thinks she will appreciate the gesture.

"Oh Emmett, I love you already, you sweet boy. I have so missed having a dog in my life. And look, now I have seven. How wonderful is that?" she asks him before she stands up. There's work to be done. Help to be given.

On the counter she sees another manila folder, this one, with her name on it. She opens it. Inside are a birth certificate, a current driver's license, a social security card, a library card and a passport for her client. She can tell they've been recently printed because of the way they smell, and the spotless condition of each item.

This is all so curious. Maybe this is how rich people live. What would she know about that? Then again, Miss Emmaline may be in a Witness Protection Program. It would explain a great deal. All the brand new things. She had no clothes, no personal effects except for the dogs. The dogs are obviously hers and have been for a while. What did her client witness? Is that why she was moved? The mob or the people wanting to kill her found out where she was and sent evil men to attack her, and so she was quickly moved and given a new identity?

It doesn't explain why Ruger is so skinny. Was he being held hostage to force her out of hiding? And when she found out where he was the evil people stopped her from taking him and brutally attacked her? What secret does she know?

Is she a criminal? Did she steal from the mob? Is she a whistle blower? Then why would she need a teacher? What terrible person would attack such a petite woman? It doesn't make any sense. It's awful and her heart breaks for Miss Emmaline, because whatever her story, she suspects it's not a happy one.

Darlene, a person of order and lifelong conformity, takes a deep breath and lets it all go. She will not ask questions. She will not worry. She will accept each day as it unfolds and be grateful for it. Grateful for a beautiful place to live, grateful for the beautiful dogs and more than enough food for everyone. A job where she can use her education, gardening skills, and imagination. She gets to live with seven well mannered pit bulls. And she doesn't have to pay for food, flea or heartworm medication. She simply gets to enjoy them. Yes, enjoy them! That's what she must do regarding this new path and these new experiences developing before her – she must enjoy it all.

"I will, Emmett. That's exactly what I shall do. I will relax, and enjoy it all. You know what else? I'll never ask Miss Emmaline anything about it. What do you think about that?"

Emmett must think it's wise and good, because he wags his tail and looks at the bright eyed smiling face of Darlene as though he has understood everything.

When Tiny wakes again the sun is shining through floor to ceiling windows directly in front of her. She sees she's in a room, but not a hospital room. She remembers a young couple finding her, stopping the attack, frantically calling 911. She remembers riding in an ambulance, the concerned expressions on the faces of the paramedics. Then nothing.

She feels the bed dip on the left side and looks over in time to see Ruger sit up, yawn widely, then stretch out the full length of his body. When he's finished, he gently licks her forehead. She reaches for his head with both of her hands, pulls his face to hers and kisses his cheek. He licks her hand, then chuffs Ruger breath in her face before leaping gracefully over her to land soundlessly on the terrazzo floor. She watches him trot happily from the room.

She's staring at the beautiful terrazzo flooring when she feels pressure on her thighs. She turns her head and sees Petal and Jasmine lying side by side, looking at her and wagging their tails in a mesmerizing rhythm. She hears a thump thump thump and looks over at a gold leather wingback chair to find Harriet wiggling and grinning and waiting for Tiny to call her over.

She smells something disgusting and familiar the instant Poof jumps on to the bed. Brownie quickly joins her. They're all soon cuddled as close to Tiny as they can get without hurting her. Harriet can't seem to stop licking Tiny's arm.

Tiny is breathing hard and it hurts her to do so, but she can't help it. The relief is too intense. The disbelief is too fearsome. This can't be real. What is this place? She pets and hugs her sisters to her as best she can. She has missed this so much. This life, this love. These wonderful pets who have been her only true family. She feels her body convulsing and she doesn't know how to stop it.

She feels her sisters move quickly away when they see Ruger charging into the room, his ears crooked in alertness, his eyes worried. Her sisters jump off of the bed when they see Ruger leaping toward it. He quickly takes their place to investigate, to check on the grand love of his life.

Ruger, her strong boy Ruger. Tiny reaches her arms up and winds them around his neck and leans all of her meager weight on him, because she knows he can take it. Her body is rocking back and forth and she cannot catch her breath. Her chest is heaving. She feels like she's suffocating. And she is suffocating. She's suffocating on her fear, her pain, her decades of silent suffering, never complaining. Never complaining about anything. Just taking it, taking whatever abuse anyone gave her. But the sight of her beautiful, healthy sisters and Ruger looking at her with such love has broken the dam.

Ruger sits close to Tiny as she holds him with all of her strength and cries out all of her anguish. She buries her face in

Ruger's thick neck and cries as she has never permitted herself to cry in her entire life. Ruger lowers his head so that Tiny's head and shoulders are cradled against his big neck and face. He loves this little human. He does not recognize the sounds she's making, but can sense a deep sadness in the loud noises. He senses he does not need to be alarmed about anything, he simply needs to be near her, as she needs to be near him.

Years of pent up anger, sadness and fear are released as sobs rack Tiny's too slender body. Slowly, mysteriously, yet most assuredly, something is released from inside her. Something that has been a terrible, invisible burden. A burden that has been too much for one person to live with, and to bear for what seems like forever. Once gone, Tiny will not allow it to return. She promises to Ruger just as she promises to herself.

As her sobs turn into hiccups, Ruger licks away her salty tears. Tiny feels her old self sloughing away, being consumed by Ruger. He's taking away all of the awful and leaving something yet to be revealed. Something different, something new, something good. The good that has always existed within her, because good is what Tiny is.

The movements of her body slowly come under her control, but her arms remain loosely wrapped around Ruger as he licks away every tear. She stays snuggled up to him for a few minutes longer. When her breath returns to its normal rhythm, Tiny feels lighter. She attempts to breathe in deeply but cannot manage it. Sharp pain paralyzes her. She reaches one hand down to feel her ribs, runs it along the secure wrapping around her ribcage and back. She recalls every instant of the attack and shudders in revulsion, but no anger. She lived with Gerald for too many years. She knows what anger does to a person. How it deforms them.

She's opening her eyes to view her surroundings when she hears the running feet of a dog. The moment she turns her head toward her bedroom door she sees Emmet bounding through it. Emmett! It can't be! But it is! There's no mistake at all. And he's gorgeous and healthy, and as innocent as when she left him. She's thinking what on earth is going on here as she watches him run toward her, and prepare to leap up onto the bed when a deep, make no mistake growl comes from Ruger. Emmett slides to a halt and crashes into the side of the bed. He knocks himself over and is scrambling to right himself when Tiny, holding on to Ruger for support, reaches down to him. She's surprised to see that he has been neutered.

"Emmett, what have you been doing, my baby boy?"

Darlene, not far behind Emmett, sees her client is awake. She also sees the special bond Miss Emmaline has with Ruger. She's about to enter and introduce herself when she hears Miss Emmaline begin to cry. Darlene quickly scoots to the wall next to the bedroom door and puts her back against it. She knows she wouldn't want to meet someone for the first time if she were crying. She doesn't want to walk away and so alert and embarrass Miss Emmaline. So she stays with her back against the wall and can't help but hear the implications of a tale of sorrow, so much so that she, too, begins to cry.

She will always remember the scene of that little bitty woman with her face buried in the neck of that huge white dog, surrounded by six Pit Bulls offering comfort and solace through their united presence.

Tiny feels herself begin to cry again as she looks at the happy face of her Emmett. He looks so good. His body is wriggling all over the place until Ruger growls low. Emmett slows down and sits down, and Tiny puts her hand on his big head and looks at his body.

"Emmett, look at you. You look so good. You've been taken care of, and I can tell by the way that you act that no one has hit you, or shocked you. You don't look like you've been living on a chain either. You don't have that fear filled submissive hunch that my sisters and Ruger had. And that I had, too, I'm sure. We were all living on chains, weren't we? But not anymore."

Tiny suddenly feels very sore and very, very tired. Her tears begin to subside as she feels Brownie and Harriet slowly worm their way behind her. She uses their bodies as a cushion to help her sit up. Emmett's head is on the bed by her hip. Poof and Petal are lying by her feet. Jasmine and Ruger are sitting side by side, Jasmine black and white, Ruger solid white. Tiny mentally counts everyone three times, once to confirm, then twice more to convince herself. She leans back on Brownie and Harriet and lets her eyes savor the delicious sight of these dogs on a king sized bed she has no idea to whom it belongs.

Ruger chuffs. Tiny looks at him sitting beside Jasmine and thinks what a pretty pair they are. She relaxes back onto Brownie and Harriet and feels them relax onto her. She breathes in as deeply as she can bear.

"Jasmine, you and Ruger sure look pretty together. Ruger, why are you so skinny, old friend? And who can tell me what's going on here? Do I want to know? Am I dreaming? Petal, my dear, if I'm dreaming, I never want to wake up. Are we prisoners?"

Darlene wipes her eyes as she listens to Miss Emmaline talk to her dogs, asking them the strangest questions. Does her client have amnesia? Before she begins to contemplate the answer, she clears her throat and walks into the room. No more eavesdropping. Introductions are in order.

Tiny looks in the direction of the noise and sees a thin middle aged white woman coming toward her. She's not alarmed because none of the dogs are alarmed. She notices the woman's approach is tentative, unsure.

She sees her red hair and the three inches of gray roots. She sees worry in her eyes, eyes looking out at her from a face exhibiting endured stress. She wonders if she looks like that: wrinkled, timid, yet hopeful.

When the woman nears her bed she looks at Tiny's family and the smile that comes to her lips transforms her face from that of tired beaten down individual who has suffered too much in too short a time into a youthful woman who could regain her confidence if she's only given the chance. Tiny smiles at her when their eyes meet again. She somehow knows that this person will change her life. And in a good way. This bedraggled looking woman is a woman of goodness. If she didn't know it, the behavior of the dogs have certainly made it clear.

"Miss Emmaline? Miss Carruthers? My name is Darlene Cauley and I'm here to help you. "

When Miss Emmaline just stares at her. Darlene begins to stutter because it dawns on her that this woman could tell her that she doesn't need help. That she's not required. This woman could ask her to leave!

"I, I, I have the ability... I know how to... We could do, I mean you can be, you can learn... I could teach you whatever you wish. We can... There is so much we..."

The woman's words trail off and she looks like she's on the verge of a panic attack. Tiny thinks she must look the exact same, because she hasn't the slightest idea who Emmaline Carruthers is.

She knew this was too good to be true.

# Chapter 12

Gerald is sitting on the sofa in his living room feeding The Qat Quartet with a syringe. The Qat Quartet have a brand new shoebox, while on his feet are new hiking shoes. He can feel the health steadily improving in their little bodies. He has learned, because he's constantly learning, because the curse of the old white woman would have driven him mad if he'd been a man of lesser intellectual ability, if he'd not been so fortunate as to have Tiny in his life, he has learned that by touching another animal he becomes privy to everything happening in their bodies and minds. He becomes aware of their emotional state as well, though he will admit that this confused him and took him the longest to acknowledge, that animals have emotions. That they feel, not only physically but, like humans, animals have responses to situations that directly affect them and those whom they care for or love.

His Crew is in the front yard. The volume on his seventy-five inch flat screen television is as loud as he can take it. He's watches, when he can bear it, but he listens attentively to every nuance of Tiny's sorrow. Beneath the sorrow that's being released into the fur of Ruger's neck, he feels relief beginning to take hold. He looks up from feeding the Qats to watch Tiny cry.

He thinks if Tiny were a cliff climber, the scene right now would be her dangling from a four hundred foot cliff with no toe holds. The tips of her callused fingers would be clinging to a two inch wide foot long ledge. She would be panicking at the great peril of her situation, but after having glanced up, she would see that the slim ledge is only six inches below the top of the steep cliff. And that all she has to do with the remaining strength in her body is reach up and pull herself over, so that she might see and enjoy the clear flowing stream beneath the shade of trees heavy with ripe fruit. Darlene would be the birdwing butterfly that flutters over her, catching her eye and making her momentarily forget her predicament by intimating there's something else to see.

On the huge UHD screen Tiny's small form shudders as she weeps into Ruger's neck. He watches Ruger move his big head so that Tiny is tucked close and protected into him. Gerald shakes his head in wonder. Ruger was painstakingly bred to be a fighter and a killer. Obviously, there's a lot more to dogs than one thinks there is. He watches the dogs, the way they interact with her, the way they comfort her.

Outside, His Crew is puzzled as they listen to a woman's voice they recognize, but the trouble filled noises are beyond their comprehension. Day decides to grab one of the toys. He wiggles it enticingly in front of his siblings until they rise to chase him across the lawn, and soon they hear nothing more but the sound of their feet on the well tended grass, their bodies crashing into one another and the playful growling and barking communication of puppy dog creatures getting along because they like the company of one another.

Gerald watches Darlene enter the room then scoot quickly back and plaster herself against the wall outside Tiny's bedroom door. He watches her wrestle with her need to comfort versus her inherent politeness which dictates she needs to wait for a better moment. He watches her listen. He watches her begin to cry.

His eyes go back to Tiny because he can't help himself. He hears her talk to Emmett, listens to her praise the dog while insulting him. But it's true what she says. The dogs and Tiny had a submissive hunch. Gerald thought that was the way all dogs looked. That getting them to that point was the goal. He'd been completely ignorant of their capabilities, even though he saw Tiny hugging and petting them when she thought he wasn't around, he had no idea that they could be companions, and until they became his companions, he hadn't fully comprehended what this word and concept meant. But then, how do you teach someone who thinks they know everything?

He likes the way the dogs feel. They're relaxed and concerned, but not worried. Like Gerald, they don't take their eyes off of Tiny. He observes the way she touches the dogs with gentleness and love. She eats them up with her eyes, looking at each one individually, then addressing each according to his or her personality and needs. The same thing she did with him. Only the way to address him had been with fearful hesitation and constant flinching. He'll admit it now, because he's constantly admitting all manner of shameful things to himself, that he thought he liked it. But he didn't. Every time Tiny flinched because of his words or actions he flinched inside, hating himself for his mistaken weakness, then quickly took his anger out on her. He was such a loser. He was a loser. Gerald's eyes widen as he speaks the final truth about himself to himself.

DARLENE LOOKS AT THE PANIC on her client's face and mistakes it for something else altogether. She mistakes it for shock of the new, of control and choices taken away from her, of her imminent termination if she doesn't act fast. The instant before she thinks her client is about to tell her to leave, Darlene asks, "Are you hungry?"

And Tiny becomes aware that, yes, yes, she is hungry. But this room, this place, is so weird and wonderful, and since all of her dreams seem to be coming true, she opens her mouth, and for the first time since she was four years old, tells this Darlene what she truly wants. If this is a dream, she's going to live it to the fullest. It goes without saying that the steady presence of all of the dogs bolsters her confidence and does much to quash her fears.

"Yes, Darlene, I am hungry. But what I'd like most of all right now, is a shower."

Darlene exhales breath she hadn't realized she was holding.

"Then that's what you shall have."

And because she doesn't know if her client has ever been in this home, she indicates with her hand while telling her,

"The bathroom is this way. Let me turn on the towel warmer, and then I can help you to the shower."

Tiny is nodding solemnly at the mention of a towel warmer as Darlene and Emmett walk away. What's a towel warmer? She can't begin to imagine what it looks like. And she can't wait to see it. She can't wait to see everything.

She tells Ruger to come closer and to stay while she pulls back the covers and swings her legs over the side of the bed. She's surprised to find that her feet almost touch the floor. This prompts her to look around the room.

The ceilings are eight feet tall. The furniture is small, retro, made for people of a smaller stature of a bygone era. Tiny knows she won't feel like a child in this furniture. She won't have to sit on the edge of the wingback to look sensible. Looking at it now, she bets that she'll be able to sit all the way back in it, and that her feet will be flat on the floor.

She asks Ruger to get down on the floor in front of her. He leaps down immediately and sits directly in front of her. She pets his head, getting ready to get up when, again, she notices the terrazzo flooring. Terrazzo flooring! It's her favorite! She gapes in wonder at the brown, gray, bronze and green spots. It's so beautiful. She looks through her bedroom door and sees that, from her position, there's nothing but terrazzo flooring. This is exactly what she would've done if she'd built a house. It dawns on her that she would have had floor to ceiling windows like this, too. And she would've liked a gold leather wingback, exactly like the one she's staring at right now.

"Ruger, this is the best dream ever. Except for the shooting pain I'm feeling all over my body, we're experiencing a perfect moment. How about you helping me to the bathroom where we'll find white marble floors and countertops, and a big soaking tub next to a large window? The shower will be a huge walk-in affair that can be entered and exited from both ends. Also, there'll be a generous teak stool inside it. And Ruger, the walls of the shower will be slab white marble while the shower floor will be white marble hexagon mosaic with dark grout. Now, help me get up before I wake up."

Tiny puts both of her hands on Ruger's wide collar and asks him to back up slowly. Ruger's eyes are on Tiny's face watching for any stress as he slowly backs up, one inch at a time.

Tiny inhales sharply when she's able to stand. The pain is intense. She feels coolness on her back and looks down. She's wearing a boxy blue hospital gown that hangs mostly away from her body. She notices a bulge above her stomach. She calls Brownie and asks her to stand near her other side because she doesn't think she can walk one step without strong support. With one hand holding onto Ruger's collar and leaning all of her weight on him she timidly touches the bulge and knows it can be nothing other than a diaper.

Her hand is shaking when she grabs a hold of Brownie's collar. She wonders if the dream will turn into a nightmare?

Darlene comes back into the bedroom to help but sees that her assistance for this task is unnecessary. She walks ahead of the threesome, marveling at the way the dogs help her client without her client saying a word to direct or correct them. Emmett is by her side while the remaining four pit bulls observe their master's progress from not too far away. Darlene can see that Miss Emmaline is in extreme pain. Yet other than attempt to telekinetically transport her to the shower, there's nothing she can do but remain close by and be ready to help if needed, considering she has no telekinetic abilities, at all.

Tiny keeps her eyes on the floor in front of her and her hands securely on the dogs' collars. Ruger slows to a stop and so does Brownie. Tiny is wondering why when she realizes the exercise has almost undone her and that the next step might have landed her on her face. She leans on Ruger until she's basically sitting on his back.

Darlene wonders if she can carry Miss Emmaline the next few steps, but fears she can't. Darlene is almost as petite as her client. She looks at Ruger, the patience of the dog so evident. She decides to follow his suit. She'll keep her mouth shut and wait.

Tiny tries to take a deep breath, but she cannot. The effort makes her chest feel as though it's on fire. How far is the bathroom? Can she make it?

As she tries to manage her pain she forgets all about Darlene. She's thinking only of, and grateful for, the strength and loyalty of Ruger. Her own very weakened physical state unnerves her. Tiny doesn't like to feel bad. She never has, no matter the cause. She doesn't waste her energy thinking miserable thoughts. She learned years ago that it served no purpose. She has the example of Gerald to thank for that.

Any slight, perceived slight, betrayal or perceived betrayal he imagined or experienced directed toward him sent him on a hyper focused trail of revenge and retribution. Sitting on Ruger's back, she remembers the times that Gerald would be days or weeks in a state of rage. Plotting and planning to get back at the individual or group who had displeased him. He would spend every waking hour thinking of ways to humiliate or defile. He had no rest. It made him miserable. He didn't eat. His body would ache all of the time. He was on a short fuse. It was not a way to live.

She remembers watching him, listening to him. He'd spend hours making and going over various elaborate revenge plans. Exploring every terrible nuance of a dark and hurtful scheme.

Tiny could clearly see the one who suffered the most was him. And she learned from this.

It was futile to live for revenge. Hate was a waste of time and was rarely justified to the extent that it was felt.

This pain is her pain. She knows what caused it was one of the vilest acts a human can perpetrate on another. It was not her fault. She did nothing to invite the violence. She had the choice to move on, or ruminate on it endlessly and make herself sick mentally, physically and spiritually. She senses something rare and possibly wonderful happening in her life at this moment. She can be afraid, or trust the unfolding. She's a different person now than she was seven months ago. Through a haze of pain, she decides she'll live in the moment, not worry or stress about the next moments, just concern herself with this moment right here.

She would lie down on Ruger's back and let him carry her to the bathroom if she thought she could endure the pain, but something tells her it'd be excruciating to attempt such a maneuver. She feels so weak, her muscles won't do what she asks them to. She reaches for Brownie, yet before grabbing her collar, pets her head. Brownie looks up at her with happy eyes, eyes that wait for Tiny. Eyes and a heart that always wait for Tiny. When Tiny gets a hold of her collar to pull herself to a standing position, a miracle occurs. It suddenly dawns on her who Emmaline Carruthers is. She is Emmaline Carruthers!

She hasn't been called that since she was three years old. Emmaline Carruthers. A name of quiet beauty. Her mother told her that Emmaline meant "peaceful home". Now as she plods slowly forward she wonders if her mother named her that because that's what she wanted most of all. She had not been able to achieve any semblance of a peaceful home on her own, so hoped naming her last born would make it happen.

Of course it did not. Tiny cannot remember one peaceful moment in her home. There was constant erratic behavior, yelling, violence, insults and persistent degrading poverty. Four able bodied adults always lived in her childhood home, yet there was never money. Perhaps because no one could be bothered to get a job. At age three when her growth seemed to stall, an "uncle" started calling her Tiny. And her family of followers, not leaders, called her that from then on. Why had her mother permitted such a demeaning name to replace such a thoughtful and lovely one? Lack of confidence, or lack of sense, or emphatically and tragically, both.

Tiny realizes she can't put all of the blame on her mother and her family, though she'd certainly like to do so. When she was old enough she could've insisted they call her by her given name. But she didn't. Like them, she waited for someone to tell her what to do. Using her mind and will as little as possible. As she shuffles impossibly slowly toward the bathroom, toward a shower, not a sponge bath, toward towels that are on a towel warmer, she thinks she's sliding toward an uncertain future, but indeed toward a new and different future. Her steps become surer as Tiny, no, as Emmaline Carruthers makes up her mind to be Emmaline Carruthers.

GERALD IS WATCHING TINY sit on Ruger's back while petting Brownie. He thinks she looks different somehow. He begins to study her like a specimen, with the detachment of a scientist trying to discover the cure for heartworms.

He sees and feels her trying to take deep breaths, but her broken ribs won't allow it. He feels her complete lack of anger. He feels her waiting, thinking. He watches Ruger stand patiently until Tiny indicates he should move. He looks at Brownie looking up at Tiny with such confident trust. There's such gentleness in her regard. Her tail wagging matches the beat of her heart. He sees the rest of The Lady Team watching with interest from the bedroom. He can feel their calmness and can be honest with himself and admit, they never felt this depth of peacefulness with him.

Once she enters the bathroom he'll be unable to see or hear her. The cameras and sound deliberately don't record in the bathroom areas. Tiny will sooner or later figure out that he's got the house wired for sound and images because he was always big on doing that at all of his properties, however, she will have a time discovering where he placed the cameras.

"But Silky, I bet she never tells Darlene," Gerald says as he places the kitten filled shoebox on the end table next to him.

Silky, Cotton and Snowball are on the sofa with him while Day and Lolly are outside on the front porch. He looks over at them. They're almost eight months old. He imagines what their lives would have been like had it not been for the old white woman.

No one would've ever noticed how beautiful they are. No one would've ever appreciated their intelligence, their curiosity and their ability to problem solve. Every day they surprise him with the depth of their intellectual capacity.

No one would've ever learned of their capacity to love, to be companions, to be a comfort to humans. They would've been sold for thousands of dollars, chained in basements and in yards. Never been allowed to touch another dog in camaraderie and never would they have felt a gentle human hand. They would've been exploited for their genetics, abused for their breed type and neglected because that's the way all of his clients treated their dogs. They treated them exactly like he treated his dogs. Monkey see, monkey do.

No more though. The dogs that come into his life from now on would be treated correctly. He'd attempt to do the same with human beings, but he doesn't know how successful he'll be. If Darlene is the test subject, maybe he'll do all right, he thinks to himself, proud of his generous salary compensations.

Gerald still has a lot to learn about humanity. Because paying someone a bunch of money to do the jobs of four people is not progress just because he's paying them, paying them for work, not for sitting around in a luxurious home drinking sweet tea by the pool. Paying her to be the nurse, cook, yard person, chicken keeper, gardener, house cleaner and pool lady. He's basically made her another Tiny except that Darlene is getting paid to be a modified slave. Compassion for his fellow man doesn't come naturally to Gerald. It may never come to him at all. Then again, it just might.

He looks back at the screen and sees the slight lift of Tiny's shoulders. He feels a difference in her. Though she's in unbearable pain, he knows because he feels every jagged nuance of it, something has transpired. Something has changed in her. He watches very closely as she shuffles the remaining steps to the bathroom. While she may be shuffling and breathing hard from the exertion of it, he could swear that she's standing taller, that her eyes are looking straight ahead. That she's comporting herself more like an Emmaline Carruthers than a woman who's always been called Tiny, and treated as such. Tiny with no last name walks into the bathroom being held up by two pit bulls.

"Silky, Emmaline Carruthers is about to re-enter the world," Gerald mutters to Silky and His Crew as he gets up from the sofa. As he walks outside onto the front porch, he notices the sun is shining on grass that's beautifully green, the sky is blue without a cloud, that there's a gentle breeze blowing. All of his dogs, his companions, are around him looking up at him, waiting to see what they're all about to do.

# Chapter 13

It's all Darlene can do to stand and keep still in the bathroom with empty hands, and watch this woman struggle to walk. She hopes her face is calm, that her posture exudes peace and confidence. She can't see how this would be possible since she's not a professional actor. Two of Miss Emmaline's Pit Bulls are valiantly supporting her as she makes her way slowly toward the shower. When she arrives at the shower entrance and places a shaking hand on the white marble for support, Darlene moves in to help.

Without words she gently takes Miss Emmaline's arm and walks her into the large shower. There's a teak stool near the handheld shower nozzle. Darlene guides her toward it.

"Miss Emmaline, why don't I help you undress? Then, if you can manage, you can shower yourself. Do you think you can? If not, I'll be just outside, sitting on the bed. You call me for anything and I'll be in here in seconds."

"Yes, let's try that. If you could turn on the water and get it steamy in here first," Emmaline says as she notices the shower has a steam function. She recognizes it because she saw it once on television. She had commented to Gerald that that'd be nice. She remembers him looking at her. She also remembers that the day after her comment, Gerald had removed the water heater on the pretense that he wanted a bigger one. But the new water heater didn't arrive for two weeks.

"What a good idea! I'll turn on the water to get the steam going. If you need assistance to turn any knob, just say so."

Emmaline nods and tries to gather what little strength she has so that she can stand while Darlene removes her hospital gown. From the corners of her eyes she watches Darlene turn the knobs. She hears the rush of strong water pressure. She sees Ruger, Petal, Jasmine and Brownie sitting inside the shower entrance. They're about four feet away from her, far enough that they won't get wet. This shower is huge. The white marble slabs are lovely. The hexagonal mosaic floor with dark grout is sublime.

Emmaline knows she is awake. This is not a dream, nor is it a nightmare. But it is surreal. The terrazzo floors, the bathroom, exactly like she saw in magazines and on television. That she showed to Gerald, exclaiming over the beauty. She remembers Gerald glancing at the images and then acting like he hadn't seen a thing. What is this new story he's creating in her life? What is he up to? Her family. This luxury and comfort. An assistant? She can't think about it now. All of her focus and strength must be on the task at hand, of bathing herself in a shower she has all to herself. She won't have to worry about anyone spying on her, waiting on her to disrobe so that they can prey on her. She hasn't had all of her clothes off to clean herself since she ran away from Gerald.

While Miss Emmaline leans on the shower wall, Darlene unties the hospital gown. As it falls to the shower floor, Darlene almost gasps aloud when she sees her back. She can see every bone there is, and her battered skin. Besides her obvious and appalling lack of nourishment, her skin is black, blue , red and yellow. Her back is covered in large colorful bruises.

Darlene gently pulls away the diaper adhesive. She does not look down because she doesn't think she can disguise her horrified expression from Miss Emmaline as she helps her sit on the stool.

She can see and feel some of the tension leave her starving body when she's seated. She watches her take a shuddering breath as she looks up at Darlene. She thinks she'll never forget the sight of that tiny battered woman, her long eyelashes surrounding soft brown eyes. Her eyes are full of gratitude and relief. Before she can speak, Darlene tells her,

"The knobs are right there. One to control the steam and the other to turn on the handheld shower nozzle. I'm sure there's enough hot water for you to stay in here for hours. You stay as long as you want, Miss Emmaline. When you're finished, after we dry you off with warm towels, we'll get you into a soft white cotton nightgown, and back into bed. After that, I will list every dish possible I can make and you can eat whatever you desire."

Emmaline closes her eyes and quietly sighs in unspoken gratitude. When Darlene reaches down to pick up the discarded hospital gown, she sees the diaper is red with blood, and that what running water has invaded it has caused blood to run in a dark red river into the drain. She exits the shower before her composure disintegrates and she humiliates herself. The dogs don't move when she passes by them as she leaves the shower.

She walks straight to the kitchen and takes a plastic garbage bag from a cabinet. She shoves the offensive garments into the bag and ties it. She then puts it into another plastic garbage bag and ties triple knots. Emmett is sitting nearby quietly watching her. He can tell his new friend is upset by her jerky movements. He watches her drop the bag on the floor, then pick it up again. She looks down at the bag and around the kitchen. Her behavior is puzzling to him. He knows something is wrong with the bag, that whatever is inside it is wrong.

"Emmett, I can tell you because I know you can keep a secret. Your MamaLady is very hurt. Bad men did very bad things to her and it has made me very very mad. I want to cry and, and, and wish terrible things upon those men. But that would make me as terrible as them. And two wrongs don't make a right? Did you see

Miss Emmaline? She's in pain. I don't know how she walked to the bathroom. Emmett, the adult diaper in this bag is full of her blood! Oh my goodness. What should I do with it? I want to burn it! I want to shred it. I want to make it, and what happened to her disappear forever. I just can't imagine what that woman went through. What she's been going through. She's literally skin and bones. Skin and bones, I tell you!"

Darlene shudders uncontrollably when she remembers the river of blood going down the drain. She knows she cannot have the offensive garments in the house. She walks into the laundry room and peers out of the long rectangle window. The trash has not yet been picked up. She dashes past Emmett to leave the bag outside with the other trash. She's putting the bag into the trashcan when she hears the powerful roar of the garbage truck. She glances up the street. The truck will be here shortly.

When Darlene turns back toward the house, she's startled to see Emmett, tall, black and beautiful, tail wagging, alert eyes on her eyes, standing right next to her. She had been without the companionship of a dog for so long she'd forgotten how they'll follow you from room to room, their utmost desire to be near you. Even now, though she was away from him for less than a minute, he looks happily up at her, excited, as if she has been gone for a day. She's tempted to grab his collar, to keep a firm hold on him until she gets him safely back inside, but her intuition tells her it's unnecessary.

She looks closely at him while he waits for her direction. She can see the Pit Bull in him, but he and his father are by far the most unusual looking Pit Bulls she's ever seen. They are tall for the breed. The musculature on their bodies is astounding. She can see no fat on either one of them. The thought crosses her mind that she would hate to be on the receiving end of their wrath, because they'd make quick work of any opponent, human or animal. Why would such a thought occur to her? She shakes it far away as they head back inside.

Ruger is ever watchful of Miss Emmaline. She's confident he's exactly where she left him, at the left end of the shower watching her every move. A gentle giant, he is. She suspects Emmett will be just as large. And with a master such as her client, he'll be as sweet and as loving as the others are. The character of Miss Emmaline shines forth in the behavior of her dogs.

She's surprised to hear how well spoken Miss Emmaline is. Her diction and inflection are like that of a professional person or teacher. Darlene doesn't know, and will thankfully never know, that Gerald corrected every incorrectly pronounced syllable or grammatical error with the precision of a busy butcher. He gave her a remarkable vocabulary because his boredom turned into secret sadism. It tickled him that she could speak like a physicist but couldn't read. Plus, she had no idea how intelligent she sounded! In this particular instance, his ill treatment of her will serve her in a beneficial manner for the rest of her life. When she's older and can consider his actions in a rational manner, she'll be grateful for the gift he unwittingly gave her.

Darlene and Emmett hustle back inside to check on Miss Emmaline. When they walk into the bathroom they see Ruger sleeping inside a steam filled space. Apparently it suits him, because Darlene can hear him snoring. The shower is still on and there's a profuse cloud of steam filling the shower and beyond. Ruger is the only dog in the shower. When he lied down and stretched himself out he must've displaced the other dogs.

All of the girls are lying or sitting on Miss Emmaline's bed. They've made themselves comfortable. Evidently very comfortable. Poof passes a monumental gaseous eruption to prove her contentment. Darlene puts her hands over her nose and grinning mouth.

She turns on the ceiling fan before she walks to the bed. They watch her, tails thumping gently on the bedding. She uncovers her mouth and nose, smiles, then slowly sits on the bed to introduce herself. As she reaches for each dangling heart name tag, she pets them and talks to them. She tells them how happy she is to be here, and how excited she is that they are here.

Petal, Jasmine, Harriet, Brownie and Poof. Gentle names given to gentle girls by a gentle and dear soul. Darlene loves each one already. She can't put into words how thrilled she is that all of these dogs are here. It gives her peace, comforts her like no human has in three year's time. They make her feel safe. She believes these dogs would not let any harm come to Miss Emmaline, Ruger most of all.

Emmaline is seated on the on the teak bench with her forehead leaning on the white marble wall of the shower. In her right hand is the shower nozzle which she lazily and repeatedly moves over her head, neck, shoulders, arms, chest, back and legs. She's enveloped in steam, her mouth open, breathing in deeper and deeper with each effort. She's not gaining a sense of strength because that's simply not possible.

The past weeks have been difficult days, filled with long hard menial work, meager wages, and expensive lodging because she was extorted by landlords due to a lack of identification and her diminutive stature. Her inability to read, the years of brutality and contempt, the absence of her sisters, her family, had stolen the pitiful amount of self confidence she recently possessed. Predators sensed it and preyed upon her. The majority of her earnings went to lodging rather than food. By the time of the attack, she was maybe eating every other day. She'd made a pact with herself that she would never again be a prostitute, so she wasn't, and she almost starved to death because of this promise.

She studies the hexagons on the shower floor as she washes the fifth application of shampoo and body wash from her hair and skin. She can see the grout has been expertly applied. There's no run over onto the white tiles. There's no more blood streaming over them either. She flexes her toes. Her toe nails are too long. They'll have to grow, wait a while longer for a clipping. She knows she can't perform the necessary movements to give her feet a civilized appearance. She looks at her fingernails on her left hand. Hard work kept them short. She places the shower nozzle back in its perch, turns her body on the bench so that she can lean her back, shoulders and head on the marble wall. It's a soothing place to be.

She looks over at Ruger who's laid out flat on the shower floor while his drowsy brown eyes watch her every move.

"I love you too, Ruger. I might not act like it, but I'm so happy, so relieved to see you, all of you. I need to tell you something though. You're too skinny, old friend. You look like me, bones poking out all over the place. Defined. We are defined, Ruger."

Ruger chuffs at the one he loves with his whole heart, then closes his eyes again. Emmaline leans back against the wall, closing her eyes as well. Dreamless dozing soon comes to them both.

Darlene listens closely from her seated position on the bed. Harriet's head is in her lap, Poof's head is on one of her shoulders. Emmett is lying on the floor by her feet. Darlene is stroking the soft fur of Brownie, who lies totally relaxed on her other side. Such a mystery this place. These dogs. This woman… Yet there is tranquility here. A lonely quietude she'll not ruin with questions but instead nurture it with care and attention. Darlene thinks she has stumbled into the opportunity of a lifetime. She's not about to spoil it with unwarranted curiosity. She pets the dogs. Stress, fatigue and worry had grown roots around her every vein, had locked themselves underneath her pores. But as she listens and pets these loving dogs she feels those roots decay, disintegrate and slowly evaporate from her person, mind and spirit. She waits patiently in the middle of six pit bulls for a noise to drift from the bathroom, a noise that will communicate the adventure is about to begin in earnest.

DAYS PASS SLOWLY as if in a dream. Darlene waits on her, takes care of her like no one ever has. Soon she can get out of the bed by holding onto just one of Darlene's hands for support. She's sore though. A soreness she knows will leave sooner rather than later. Darlene has walked her to a chair on the back covered patio. She's settled into one of the deep cushioned loveseats. Poof steps up to join her. Ceiling fans overhead stir the air, pushing a soft breeze around where otherwise one wouldn't exist.

This is the first time she has been outside. While she sits quietly in her nightgown considering her new surroundings, Ruger and Emmett roll around on the green grass. The neutering of Emmett makes her wonder what this indicates about Gerald. She almost begins to think about him, then stops herself.

Petal walks round and round on an elevated bed until the requisite number of circles are completed that will ensure true comfort. Emmaline watches her settle, glance over at her, then sigh deeply. Darlene smiles at Petal and turns to Miss Emmaline to make a comment, but pauses when she notices the faraway look in her eyes. Instead, she follows her gaze to Ruger and Emmett and the beautiful yard. To the white crepe myrtles that look like angelic sentries around the perimeter of the white vinyl fencing. There are red cardinals on the ground beneath them and blue birds perched on the branches. This morning she filled the bird feeders that arrived yesterday afternoon. Four different designs for four different types of feed.

Over the course of the past days, Darlene has done her best to get Miss Emmaline past this unfortunate time in her life. She has discovered that the woman is the kindest, most patient human being she has ever met. Not once has she complained of her physical discomfort, or tried to place any greater burden on Darlene. She's sharp, well spoken, and has the manners of a lady.

Darlene can see every bone in her body. Her face looks like a skeleton. Her natural instinct is to feed her steak, eggs and well buttered cheesy mashed potatoes three times a day. She knows this would do more harm than good, because like a dog who has been deliberately starved to death, the reacquainting period to food must proceed with small incremental portions that are judiciously timed. The food cannot be rich or force the body to work hard to digest.

Miss Emmaline eats a soft fried egg in the morning with half a piece of wheat toast, along with hot tea and lemon, instead of creamed sugar coffee. A small bowl of brothy soup for the mid-morning snack, broiled fish and steamed vegetables for lunch, then fruit for the afternoon snack, and then... Nothing. Miss Emmaline has said she couldn't eat supper, that she had no room for it.

When Darlene looks again at Miss Emmaline she's petting Jasmine, Poof and Brownie. Harriet, like Petal, is asleep on one of the elevated beds. She's smiling as she watches Ruger and Emmett wrestle and run on the large lawn.

"It's a beautiful day. I think I'll mow the lawn this morning," Darlene says.

"Where's the lawnmower?" Emmaline asks her.

"In one of the sheds, through that arch there, in the fence," Darlene says as she points to an arch covered in vines coated with small yellow flowers.

"Mow the yard? Yes, I think you're right. It's time for that. And time for something else, too. Time for someone to get a move on. Time to have a look around. Come here, Ruger. Come help me get going."

Darlene is on the verge of getting up to help her when Emmaline says,

"You stay right there, Darlene. You're doing so much for me. Just take a look at my pretty pink toenails!"

Darlene smiles and looks down at Miss Emmaline's bare feet. She watches her wiggle toes that boast bright fuscia colored nails, pedicured to perfection. Darlene laughs out loud, not only at the comedic gesture, which is wonderful to behold, but also at the remembrance of the long toenails, the cracked skin on her feet. Now her delight erupts in laughter to see the lovely color on perfectly shaped toenails that sit in smooth, well oiled skin. They both remember the awful which is turning into the lovely, and their happiness at the sight and feel can only be expressed in laughter.

When Emmaline and Ruger re-emerge, albeit slowly, she's dressed neatly in brightly patterned yoga pants, a lime green t-shirt with the head of a grinning white pit bull on it, white athletic shoes and socks, a wide brimmed hat, and a pair of sunglasses from the ten pair of the most interesting looking sunglasses that arrived this morning by express delivery. These frames are in the shape of large daisies with green tinted lenses.

"You look like you're ready to garden!" exclaims Darlene.

"Well, I'm certainly not going to mow this lawn. Too much jostling."

"Then you can see to the chickens, if you wish."

Emmaline's eyes widen in surprise, but the large frames hide the reaction from Darlene. Chickens! She has always wanted chickens.

# Chapter 14

Once certain that Darlene is concentrating and whole heartedly focused on mowing the lawn behind the house, Emmaline turns, takes off her daisy sunglasses and stares at what's before her. The fenced raised beds, the chicken pen, the sheds, and then, the pecan orchard to her right. When she squints her eyes, she thinks she can see another building tucked into the far back corner.

What is this? She remembers seeing the mirror images of this layout on television. She remembers telling Gerald what a dream it would be to have this, that this set up could produce more than enough food for the two of them, that he could make money! They could start with five chickens and one raised bed, she would show him how it could be done.

The next week he had moved them to a crummy condominium with a concrete patio for five months, and only allowed gardening and livestock channels to be watched on the television. When he moved them to the next house with a large yard, she never said another word about growing anything.

What game is he playing? Emmaline gathers the dogs to her because what she sees and what she's remembering is giving her the heebie jeebies. They sense her nervousness and stay close without any further command.

What's happening is surreal. It cannot be real. But there's Ruger, there are the girls, and she saw Emmett get on the zero turn mower with Darlene. She doesn't understand. There has been so much kindness and gentleness, more in her life than ever before. She knows she's shaking uncontrollably when she steps forward to investigate. She looks down to make sure Ruger is right beside her. His eyes meet hers. She sees no worry or concern in his. They all move forward slowly.

She walks slowly past the fully fenced raised gardens because she wants to see the chickens.

She and her family stand quietly in front of the wall of chicken wire. She solemnly watches the chicks scurry and murmur in the enclosure. She visually determines that there's room for more birds. Plenty more room. She sees that the coop and the buildings on either side of it were constructed with expertise and consideration. She knows a little about raising chickens due to the five month 24/7 livestock television marathon, but probably not enough. Or maybe she does. It's about to be found out exactly what she does know. She gets the impression that Darlene knows even less than she. When Darlene's eyes had strayed to the raised beds, Emmaline could tell she wanted to get her hands into the dirt rather than mow.

Darlene had shown her where she'd planted tomatoes, okra and peppers. She told her she had to force herself to wait to plant the rest, especially the Three Sisters planting. Emmaline had nodded because she didn't know what else to do, and was so glad the large frame sunglasses hid what was surely a monumentally dumbfounded look on her face.

She listens to the strong purr of the lawnmower as she investigates yet another wonder this house is offering up. Her growing excitement squashes her trepidation, and gives her a boost of energy, while the dogs give her confidence.

Inside the large shed there's another zero turn lawnmower. Of course there is. Behind the lawnmower there's a door that leads to another connected area of the shed. Emmaline and the dogs walk through it to discover a forty foot long twenty foot wide glass roofed greenhouse. She stands in the doorway with her hand on Ruger's head, and her mouth open. To her immediate left is a wall of shelves with boxes and bags of every type of fertilizer and pest deterrent any professional gardener would ever need.

In the middle of the greenhouse is a ten foot wide swath of rich dark soil. Along the sides of the greenhouse are wooden slatted potting areas. There are planting wells or tubs, she's not sure what to call them, three feet wide and three feet deep filled with the rich earth. They walk over to one of the ten. The dogs are relaxed, smelling here and there, investigating in peace. No varmint alerts.

She sees a built in watering system on the ceiling and on the walls. She and the dogs walk down the length of the greenhouse. She runs her hands over the unused surfaces, digs her fingers into the soil, where surely, anything planted will grow with vigor. When they arrive at the back of the custom greenhouse structure, she finds a large sliding barn door. Without hesitation she slides it back and sees that directly behind the greenhouse, beneath towering pine trees tilting back and forth in the wind, is a large multi-use area. Various wooden bins have been constructed. There are also hay bales set in large U formations for composting as well. She sees two water hydrants.

On her right is the back of the chicken area. With her left hand absent mindedly petting Ruger's head, she thinks that even if the chicken area is expanded, there will remain ample room for the lawnmower or a truck to get in and out to haul whatever is necessary.

Her mind becomes alive with ideas and plans of doing things in the dirt and with poultry, imaginings she has had since she can remember. Then abruptly, like an ice bath thrown over her, thoughts full of promise cease. Tiny stands perfectly still, thinking, shakes her head and says to herself, No, not Tiny. You're Emmaline, Emmaline Carruthers. She asks herself, what would an Emmaline do in this situation? Action answers the question.

She turns around, closes the well oiled sliding barn door, walks down the long length of the marvelous greenhouse until she comes to the area where there are bags of onion and garlic bulbs to be planted, along with cucumber, squash and zucchini plants. The dogs stand beside her, tails wagging and eyes watching.

Brownie licks her hand before she and her other sisters leave the greenhouse to walk through the storage shed. She watches them settle in for naps in front of the gate to the raised garden area. She feels Ruger push on her from behind, moving her closer to the plants on the counter. She looks down at him. Her big boy is looking up at her with his tongue hanging out, joy in his eyes and a smile only a Pit Bull can smile.

"Ruger, you're absolutely right. What are we waiting for?"

Grinning now, Emmaline turns to fetch one of the small woven metal wagons so she can fill it with plants and make yet another dream come true. If it's all taken from her tomorrow, then so be it. Right now, in this moment and the following few, she will plant vegetables as though she and Darlene will be the ones to harvest and consume them.

When Darlene and Emmett ride through the flower covered archway they see Miss Emmaline perched on the edge of one of the raised beds. She has pink garden gloves on her hands. Darlene slows the mower to watch her dig holes with a purple handled trowel, then gently, almost reverently, move the small plants and bulbs to their best places and proper distances. As she turns the mower toward the back acreage, she looks down at Emmett and knows she's smiling, laughter bubbling up in her again.

When the last garlic bulb is buried, Emmaline removes the garden gloves. Ruger rises from his prone position to walk over to her and put his head on her lap. She looks down at him as she puts her hand on his head. Her hand is so small compared to his head. At the sound of his name from her lips his tail starts lightly thumping the earth.

"Ruger, I just planted vegetables for the first time in my life. I always thought I'd enjoy it, but it's much more profound than that. These little bulbs you see here in my hand, these little plants, given the right conditions will flourish and grow to their full potential, as they were meant to."

Emmaline pauses to consider the bulb, the plants, and her remarkable surroundings.

"Would you please take a look at this set up? You won't remember because you were a prisoner and a slave in the back yard at the time, but I saw this exact design on television. It was on a half hour program. There was this gentleman who was a world renown gardener. He'd written books, taught at universities, and eventually had his own television show dedicated to helping people turn their yards into edible gardens. Most of the families were poor and uneducated. You could tell by the number of children they had and their haircuts, and by how exhausted they looked, the black circles under worried eyes. You ever notice that rich people seldom look tired? Does it matter, Ruger? Does the story I'm telling you matter? I don't know. But I feel compelled to tell it to you, so please be patient."

Ruger chuffs his assent.

"Thank you, darling. This family of six, husband, wife and four children under the age of six lived in a small two story home on one and half acres. There was a stream running through the middle of the back yard. The family had inherited the home and property from the husband's grandfather. I think the grandfather knew what he was doing, because though they wore thrift store clothes and his wife cut his hair, and there were dark circles under his eyes from long grinding hours of work at a sunless factory, the young man had dignity and presence. Both he and his wife did. There was an honest and humble regard in his eyes as they listened to the famous gardener talk. It had been the wife's sister who'd sent their story in, unbeknownst to them.

"You guessed it! They were chosen for the do over. When the famous gardener and his camera crew arrived and surprised the family on a rare day off, you could tell the wife was not pleased, that the husband was tired beyond words, but his upbringing and character dictated that he welcome the strangers. Neither of them had ever heard of the famous gardener because they didn't have the time or money for a television.

"The famous gardener wasn't famous for nothing. You could see he immediately assessed the discomfort of the family and that they didn't want him to film or come inside. The next shot was of them all standing in the weed choked back yard. One good thing, the acreage was completely fenced.

"Long story short, he helped them transform a large part of their yard into a vegetable garden, whereby they'd have enough food to eat themselves, and plenty left over to sell. The famous gardener also designed an area for play, and supplied playground equipment.

"Long story shorter and the end, the famous gardener and his camera crew returned to visit the family two years later. The difference was amazing. The couple were smiling, they and their children were literally glowing with health and vitality. The family had discovered, to their infinite delight, that they were natural famers, good at growing things. And that they absolutely loved it.

"Poof, I can smell that all the way over here. I'm almost finished.

"So Ruger, you know what they did? Because someone was kind to them, just kind for no reason at all, they transformed almost the entirety of their acreage into a farm. The husband was working part time and told the famous gardener that if all went as planned, he'd be able to quit his job within the year. They believed the farm would be profitable enough by then. The famous gardener laughed and said he had no doubt that it would exceed all of their expectations. He was so happy for them. He also brought gifts on that day. Can you guess what he brought? He brought thirty chicks that would grow into laying hens, builders, and the materials for a chicken coop and shed. And you know what? It looked exactly like this. Exactly. The design, the dimensions, the materials, everything. The only difference in this set up, is they didn't have that fancy greenhouse with the glass paneled roof. But everything else looked exactly like what you see here. Kind of gives you the heebie jeebies, if you let it. Or, there's one other way to consider all of this.

"The young couple accepted not only the gift of the famous gardener's knowledge and expertise, they also accepted his material gifts. They hadn't asked for anything, hadn't expected anything, but when it came, they didn't fold their arms across their chests and look away with stiff necked pride. They opened their arms, their hearts and their minds to everything that man was willing to give them. And they transformed their lives and their future because of their humility. Ruger, if I could read and work a computer, I could look them up and show you. I bet their farm, and their family, is thriving today. I wish I knew how to show you."

Emmaline and Ruger are walking to the gate of the raised garden area when Darlene and Emmett drive up and into the shed. Emmaline follows them inside. Emmett leaps from the mower to greet them. Darlene turns the mower off and looks at Miss Emmaline, at the dogs around her.

"Miss Emmaline, if one must mow acres of land, this is the way to do it. This machine is so much fun to drive. You're going to love it!"

Emmaline chuckles and says, "I'm sure I will."

The two ladies walk out of the shed and begin an interesting conversation on vegetable gardening. Darlene wants to know what Emmaline planted and where, so they walk back into the raised garden area. This time all of the dogs accompany them. Darlene praises Emmaline on her choice and location of plantings. They move among the beds, sharing thoughts and ideas. Darlene points to two of the beds that seem to have an extra concentration of sunlight bearing down on them.

"That's where we should plant the three sisters, in those two beds. Have you ever heard of the three sisters planting?"

When Emmaline shakes her head, Darlene proceeds to tell her the story of the Three Sisters.

"When Native American people speak of the "Three Sisters," they refer to corn, beans, and squash. These plants are known as the sustainers of life, and are the basic foods of sustenance. They're seen as three beautiful sisters because they grow in the same mound in a garden. The corn provides a ladder for the bean vine. The squash vines shade the mound and hold moisture in the soil for the corn and beans. The well-being of each crop planted is said to be protected by another. Legends vary from tribe to tribe but the legend of "Three Sisters" originated when a woman of medicine could no longer bear the fighting among her three daughters. She asked the Creator to help her find a way to get them to stop. That night she had a dream, and in it each sister was a different seed. In her dream, she planted them in one mound in just the way they would have lived at home. She told them that in order to grow and thrive they would need to be different but dependent upon each other. They needed to see that each was special and each had great things to offer on her own, and with the others. The next morning while cooking breakfast, she cooked each daughter an egg, but each was different: one hard-boiled, one scrambled, and one over-easy. She told her daughters of her dream and said to them, "You are like these eggs. Each is still an egg but with different textures and flavors. Each of you has a special place in the world and in my heart." The daughters started to cry and hugged each other. Now they would celebrate their differences and love one another more because of them. From that day on, Native American people have planted the three crops together—Three Sisters helping and loving each other."

Emmaline is quiet when Darlene finishes speaking. Darlene doesn't know her client well enough to tell that she has been deeply moved by the story. Strife and petty anger replaced by enduring love and support. She recalls the story she told Ruger and compares the two.

When love, kindness and respect show up, everything changes. Her thoughts turn to Gerald. She knows he built this. And that he didn't do it in kindness or love. She has never seen him be kind to anyone or anything and doesn't know if he's even capable of it. She does know that something life altering has occurred in his life. So much so that what he intended for a hate filled taunt has turned into just the opposite.

The house and grounds took years to develop and mature. But her clothes, her shoes, the sunglasses, those were thoughtful, spontaneous gifts chosen with care and tenderness. Something has happened to him. She has decided that, like the young couple, she will accept his gifts. This doesn't mean she trusts him. The dogs will protect her now. Their loyalty is to her and she need never fear him again as long as they are with her. She doesn't want to see him. She doesn't want to think about him either. But how can she not?

"Did you like the story? Do you want to plant the Three Sisters?" Darlene asks hesitantly because Miss Emmaline is so quiet.

"Darlene, I loved the story. So much beauty, so much depth. I can't wait to plant the Three Sisters. I will never think of corn, squash and beans in the same way ever again. Thank you for sharing that with me."

"Miss Emmaline, there's something else I'd like to share with you as well. I was hired to do all of these other things, but the main reason I was hired is to assist you in your education. I was a teacher for almost thirty years. That's my calling – teaching. And my contractual agreement with my employer is that I stay here as long as I make a direct and definitive impact on your learning, your education. That's the deal. You learn, I get to stay."

"What could you teach me?" Emmaline asks, unsure of what this means, but unable to still her racing heart.

"What would you like to learn?" asks Darlene, not knowing or having a clue as to what Miss Emmaline's response will be.

Emmaline pauses, removes her sunglasses, looks Darlene in the eyes, feels Ruger, Emmett, Harriet and Jasmine leaning against her, and is glad of it because she feels faint. She thinks this is one of the most important moments of her life and she doesn't want to blow it. She takes a deep breath and says,

"I want to learn to read."

Darlene feels her jaw drop but she flat out can't help it.

"You can't read?"

"No. I don't know how to read."

Darlene wants desperately to think of her client, but her weak mercenary human nature overcomes her. She can't stop thinking that she'll get to live here for years, continue to make this crazy amount of money, earn the outrageous bonuses because her gut tells her that once Miss Emmaline starts learning, she'll never want to stop. It's wild! It's, it's...

"Why, that's wonderful!"

Both ladies are surprised by Darlene's uncensored honesty. Emmaline is the first to start laughing, with Darlene soon joining her. Not to be outdone with so much joy, Poof expels a championship gaseous eruption that if one had a lit match, the entire surroundings would've been aflame in moments. Laughter turns to giggling as Darlene and Emmaline wave wildly at the air in front of them in a futile gesture to push away the epic putrid stench.

# Chapter 15

Gerald is impressed with the manner in which Darlene takes charge. He likes the way she involves Tiny in all of her educational planning. The empty shelves on either side of the fireplace soon begin to fill with books on chickens, vegetable gardening, pool care, cookbooks, old time beginner readers, elementary math books which soon graduate to high school level, books on geography, science, books related to school learning and books related to life learning.

Darlene had asked her where she wanted to begin, what her first goal would be other than learning how to read. Darlene had handled the delicate and awkward subject with such straightforward professionalism that he could see Tiny wasn't embarrassed. Tiny had replied without hesitation that she wanted to study for her GED. Out loud, Gerald tells the syringe nursing Qat Quartet that he'd already taken the GED for her, and passed it for her as well. The Qat Quartet, eyes beginning to open, remain silent and healthy in their cozy shoe box. Lolly, Day, Snowball, Cotton and Silky sleep through most of his one sided conversations.

When the women turn the living room into a workout room, he does the same. Like them, he pushes the furniture against the walls. When they do yoga, so does he. When they do Pilates, so does he. When he discovers kettle bells, he orders three complete sets, two for them, one for himself. He doesn't realize he's smiling when they receive them and endeavor to discover what they are without the enclosed visual aid.

Darlene has assigned all research to the now high school level reader Tiny. The computer from Tiny's office has been moved to the kitchen; the dining area has become the classroom. He watches Tiny peck slowly at the keyboard as she tries to match the kettle bells to images and information online. He likes that they live in the kitchen. The keeping room has become their den. There's plenty of room for all of the dogs to lie on the floor, various elevated beds, or furniture if they choose. Gerald is startled when Tiny squeals in delight when she discovers the use for the heavy oddly shaped objects.

One thing puzzles him though – she has declined to leave the house. He knows Darlene is aware of the vast amounts of available monies for their discretionary use. He has watched and listened as she has repeatedly tried to coax Tiny to go out to eat, to go bowling, to go to the park, or just to ride around town with all of the dogs. He thought that would happen when she saw the brand new SUV he bought for her. It was not only loaded to the gills with every reasonable amenity, but the rear portion had been modified to accommodate the dogs, both for their comfort and their accidents.

He had observed Tiny getting into the $90,000 vehicle with Ruger. He switched to the SUV camera and watched her run her hands over the supple orange leather seats while appreciating the oversized sunroof and absence of rear seating. He heard her when she commented how nice it was that there was no carpet on the floor. Gerald is nodding, mentally patting himself on the back for thinking of everything. Yet she still won't leave the house.

At the end of four months, Tiny finally has her intellectual breakthrough. She begins listening to herself read instead of hearing herself read. Darlene is across from her on the other side of the kitchen island peeling a bumper crop of tomatoes she's prepping for homemade sauce when she hears Miss Emmaline's voice take on a different tenor. She stops what she's doing and looks up at her.

Gerald, who'd been managing his ever increasing empire from two military grade laptops with security encryption he designed and was confident was hack proof, stops when he detects a change in the noise pattern. He looks at the screen, watching and listening to Tiny as she reads. When he looks over at Darlene, he notices she's frozen in place, her hands paused in the middle of a slicing action. He sees she's staring at Tiny. The UHD pixelation allows him to make out the expression of surprise on her face. He quickly zooms the cameras to close-up and switches the screens until he can see each woman from three different angles. There are now six smaller screens on the big screen tv enabling him to observe every nuance of each facial expression on both women. He also increases the volume so he can hear what Darlene has heard.

Initially, he can't figure out what it is. Tiny is reading from a high school history text. He looks over at Darlene to see she remains frozen in position, but there's excitement in her eyes. What is it? What's up? What's different? He turns from his laptops to give his full attention to whatever momentous change has occurred.

Then he hears it. The change in the timber of her voice and the manner in which she's reading. She no longer stumbles or hesitates over words. There's no painstaking struggle to utter words she speaks every day but could never read. There's a fluidity to her efforts now. He, like Darlene, becomes frozen in place. His eyes dart to Tiny's face. He watches her read and can't help but be... be what? Happy for her? Proud of her? Happy and proud for her? What does he feel? Does he feel anything at all? If he's completely honest with himself, what he feels is anger. He's mad. He's mad because the more learned Tiny becomes, the less she will need anyone. Education will make her an independent woman. If he had any doubt that he was out of her life, he knows that soon, she will no longer need him for anything at all. If she moves from this home, she'll be out of range of his spying devices. She'll be completely out of his reach.

Then he recognizes what he feels is not anger, but misery.

GERALD BEGINS TO NOTICE a subtle difference in his thinking and energy levels. He's in the forest with His Crew when he sees two pileated woodpeckers fly close by him. They fly so close he thinks he could've touched them. They fly onto the trunks of a forking tree thirty feet away and peck away at the bark. After a minute or two, they fly away off into the forest. He's surprised by the size of them. He hadn't realized they were so big. The red caps on the tops of their heads are a bright bright red, making them look both fearsome and fun. He wonders if they're playing or mating.

His eyes travel up the trees to their leafy boughs. He watches the leaves change color as each side is exposed to sunlight when the breeze turns them up and over. Suddenly, he's acutely aware of his surroundings. He notices the bark on the trees, the wild flower vines blooming where they can, butterflies, dragon flies, and birds feeding where they will.

The sound of man is absent. His Crew wait for his leadership. Strong muscles are forming on their bodies, and his, from the regular daily exercising. They have energy to spare. He stays extra active because of them. His recently implemented weight lifting regime has helped increase his endurance. They can walk for hours, and some days they do.

He sees bees buzzing around clover. He stands perfectly still as he watches them feed. He's acutely aware of His Crew and turns his full attention to them. Lolly, Day and Silky are standing near him smelling the air. Lolly's eyes are half closed. Day's ears are up, alert to any irregular noise or movement. Day, like Lolly, is a natural watch dog. Gerald didn't know that existed.

He thought all dogs were exactly alike but could be trained to perform certain tasks. He was wrong about that, as he was wrong about everything related to dogs.

When Day and Lolly hear a noise their response is different from the rest of His Crew. They become quiet, listen with a heightened awareness which Snowball, Cotton and Silky aren't interested in augmenting or honing. Lolly's sense of hearing is off of the charts while Day's eyesight is beyond superb. The two of them are aware of each other's strengths, but instead of competing, they use each other's unique skills to better protect Gerald, his environment and their territory. All of His Crew possess the remarkable two hundred twenty million olfactory nerves canines are born with, compared to the measly five million of humans.

He feels the extra alertness of Lolly and Day while he feels the total relaxed and peaceful states of The Lookalikes. Silky smells to experience, not investigate or protect. Gerald knows if he continues to stand still, she'll join her sisters, and like them, lie down on the pine straw covering the ground until play or sleep take over. Day and Lolly don't really rest on their walks; their personalities and drive don't give them a choice. They constantly scan their surroundings with their eyes and noses, and when curiosity and scent dictate, their mouths.

Gerald knows they love him more intensely than The Lookalikes. They watch him more closely and they seem to be always near him, unless they determine they need to perform a perimeter check. Other than those times, they seem to be beside him whenever he looks down.

The reason he knows they love him more is because he feels the interest in them more deeply than the others. If Day and Lolly are sleeping when he leaves the room, he can sense the moment one or the other opens their eyes because he feels a sense of loss. When Day and Lolly can't see him, they're sad. It's not a deep sadness, rather an unsettled feeling that's not distress, not worry, but they miss him, they long for him when they can't see him. The Lookalikes enjoy him, love him, feel a desire to protect him, yet their sentiment for him is a shallow stream compared to the depthless regard and admiration Day and Lolly feel for him.

He doesn't understand why they feel more deeply than the others. But they do. It's true. It's yet another testament to the fact that each dog is unique. Day and Lolly love him more but even the way they love him, the way they express a desire for his companionship and touch is different for each one. Day likes to be petted when he asks for it. Lolly must sleep with him.

Gerald had never shared his bed with anyone in his entire life. He gave into Lolly because she insisted on it with cute timid grunting, and when that didn't work, loud senseless panting, and when those two methods failed, a low keening noise that gave the impression her heart was breaking. And in fact, it was, because if she didn't get to sleep with him it hurt her feelings; she'd give him the cold shoulder until he gave in. Which he did. He gave in to all of them. He gave in with abandon once he realized helping and giving was not a sign of weakness, but actually the surest sign of strength. To serve, to help, is to live.

In the forest he looks down at Day and Lolly and it's almost as if they're speaking to him with words. By the look in their eyes, the tilt of their heads, their confident stances, he knows exactly what they're communicating.

'We're happy to be here, to wait with you forever but we'd like to know when more walking and running will occur."

The Lookalikes are speaking more with one another than with him. Snowball is wagging her tail back and forth while sniffing and licking clover. She knows her tail is thump thumping on Cotton's back. Cotton is lying down beside her watching her sniff and lick the clover and waiting to see if it will turn into food which she will pounce on. Silky has walked towards her sisters to see what they're doing and to make sure they aren't playing without her. Because if they're playing, she'll have to play, too.

This is infinitely more exciting than standing alert forever. Day and Lolly can handle the standing alert. Cotton and Snowball look at her and chuff, exactly like Ruger does. It communicates the same thing as when he does it,

"Come over closer. We want you to be with us."

It is exquisite. This manner of existing he had no idea was even possible. It's a luxurious feeling knowing that intelligent, strong, multi-faceted creatures care for him. In the past months, as he has watched them grow, he has learned to respect them. He learns it every moment he's with them. He looks down at Day and Lolly, who stand on either side of him like sentries, who look up at him the instant he lowers his head because they're so attuned to him physically, he glances over at The Lookalikes who're rolling on the ground in a gentle well-muscled ball trying to get the one clover stalk that's hanging from the side of Snowball's grinning mouth and he thinks this is the way to live: to be consciously aware of everything going on in your life at the exact moment it's happening.

He knows this hyper awareness is accessible to him due to Tiny's excitement and the success of her education. The clarity in his thinking and thoughts is happening because of what Tiny is living and embracing with a joy filled enthusiasm which he feels just as much as she does. Since he has never felt this, he's convinced that pristine mental clarity is only possible when no harm is occurring. No thoughts to harm another, no physical harming of another and no psychological harming of another. No lies, no insults, no manipulations. He also believes that living in the present moment is key to mental clarity. Not living for a future that may never happen, or wallowing in a past that can't be altered.

When he feels his mind moving forward or backward, the clarity is greatly reduced. And this mental clarity is one of the most wondrous experiences he's known. If all he has to do to maintain the phenomenal, almost effortless, focus and awareness is not think of the future or dwell on the past, he'll do it. It's absolutely worth it. To feel this alive, well, he never wants it to end. And it won't if he can help it, which he's convinced he can.

He breathes in deeply, smells the clean smells. He looks up to see, and to feel, the breeze moving the leaves and smaller branches. He becomes aware of the caress of the light air on his face. He looks at His Crew and feels their contentment, interest, and trust. He exhales completely and focuses on the Qat Quartet, feels them sleeping soundly in their custom shoebox. He stretches his arms high above his head and admires his new muscles and flexibility. He squats deeply, knowing that when he does so, Day and Lolly will lean into him. Does he squat to feel the health and strength in his body? Or is it because he needs a hug? Has new Gerald learned to love? He wonders if he's even capable of it.

The breeze intensifies and becomes a wind. As Gerald stands he takes a step forward, then another and another. Soon he's walking briskly down cleared paths he no longer has to mow or manicure. His feet and the feet of His Crew have pounded down the unruly vegetation. All that remains are winding trails with excellent views on all sides. It's up to him to choose which one he wants to travel in this present moment.

EMMALINE CARRUTHERS SAILS through her high school GED examination. Her hard work, her discipline, and her hunger for learning earn her scores in the ninety-eighth percentile. Darlene, who can't stop grinning, watches her student read her test scores again and again. She can't decide who's more excited, she or Miss Emmaline. Darlene looks at this woman who, over the last year, has become a dear and trusted friend.

It had been a challenge to design a program of study for an adult who couldn't read yet possessed profound intellectual abilities along with an unmatched thirst for knowledge. Her innocent wonder and appreciation for learning had thoroughly reignited Darlene's passion for teaching. She had so long been in a school system where students every year cared less and less about learning due to their obsession with themselves. Young people's faces were more often buried in their phones on social media rather than in books and nature.

She loved that there were no senseless time wasting committee meetings. Her phone didn't ding constantly with text messages informing her of nothing. It has been the most liberating experience of a lifetime, to work in this peaceful but highly driven and ambitious atmosphere.

Her only concern is that Miss Emmaline has not left the house. Darlene ceased her suggestions. She had confidence that Miss Emmaline would leave when she was ready. An individual who possessed not only intelligence but level headed reasoning would soon come to the conclusion that it was unreasonable and unhealthy to live the unnecessary life of a shut-in. Darlene waited silently and patiently for her to make the decision to leave the house. She knew she would when she was ready.

Every day, weather permitting, while Miss Emmaline worked in the garden and tended to the chickens, Darlene and Emmett went for a long walk in the neighborhood. Emmett, though technically Miss Emmaline's dog, had chosen Darlene as his forever person. He followed her everywhere she went, even to the bathroom. He slept on an elevated bed in her bedroom because he was too hot natured to sleep in the king size bed with her, though sometimes he would nap while she read at night before turning in. But when she turned the light off and rolled over under the covers, he jumped off of the bed and onto his, which was only an arm's length away.

Darlene never tried to make Emmet her own. He did it all by himself. For some reason, he loved her best and wanted to be with her always. This wonderful, glorious choice by Emmett aided in healing Darlene's broken heart, from the absence of her husband, and her broken spirit, which working in an institution will do to any sane person.

She looks down at him and likes that his head comes to her hips. His solid black coat is sleek and shiny from regular baths and good nutritious food. If he weren't her dog and she didn't know what a kind playful nature he possessed, she'd be terrified of him if she saw him coming toward her. He's unmistakably a Pit Bull, but his size and musculature are unusual and weird. Though she's accustomed to the way he looks, when she sees others cross the street on their walks, she'll look down at him and see him as they do. As an intimidating and dangerous animal capable of terrific and permanent destruction.

He has the square Pit Bull head and the large mouth that seems to have had smiling uppermost in mind when it was designed. He has the short haired coat of the Pit Bull. He has the medium sized ears that flop over, but perk up when he's excited, then fan back when he's delighted. He has the long slender tail of the Pit Bull. His body type and legs are similar to the breed but Emmett and Ruger's bodies are different from any Pit Bulls she's ever seen. Their chests are huge and wide and covered in thick rippling muscles. And though their bodies taper slightly to their rears, they have muscles like none she's ever seen on a Pit Bull. Their legs are larger than normal, too. They must be to bear the weight of all of the muscles and might in their bodies.

As Emmett walks placidly beside her, he has no idea of the stir he causes. She likes that he makes such a meaningful impression. It means that their walks are quiet, undisturbed and perfect for contemplation. Her contemplation is gratitude filled. Her contemplation is relaxed and meandering but grounded in the present moment. The happiness and wonder Emmett feels every single time they go for a walk infects her, and slowly, without even being aware of what's happening, changes her entire perspective on life.

As they walk along curving sidewalks under far reaching oaks, beside fragrant flowers and trees, next to hummingbirds and butterflies, Darlene gains a new awareness of life. The powerful intimidating presence of Emmett allows her to completely relax and regroup. At the end of the year, she's slimmer, stronger and more mindfully fit than she's ever been in her life. Plus, what's more wonderful than being with a great guy who adores you every second of every day?

# Chapter 16

Emmaline notices that Petal is not acting her usual self. Each day she seems more and more fatigued. This afternoon she's seated on the floor beside where Petal is lying down on her side. She's petting her head, shoulders and her back. Petal is lying on the floor beside her bed. She has been in the same place since last night. She doesn't seem to have the energy to get up. Emmaline strokes her head and looks at a white muzzle and face that was once solid gray. She doesn't want to admit it, but she knows what's happening.

Petal's body, long used and abused, tethered to a six foot length of a too heavy chain as soon as she could walk, is on the verge of giving out. Emmaline knows she will probably pass away soon. She has not wanted any food or water in almost forty-eight hours. For the past two weeks Emmaline watched as her health declined. She knew there was no cure. She knew that all she could do was make her passing from this world into the next as comfortable as possible.

As she strokes her beloved sister she can't help but think of her last litter and the previous nine. She had helped, when she could, when she could sneak away to her, she had helped Petal bring forth into the world seventy healthy babies. She is absolutely sure that the only survivors are the last six. The rest were used, abused, tortured, murdered and slaughtered by individuals who had absolutely no regard for life. It breaks her heart to think of this as she comforts this beautiful girl who has been her friend, confidante, and family member. She can't stop the tears from rolling down her cheeks as she thinks of Jasmine, who has already begun showing signs of slowing down forever, too.

When Darlene and Emmett come into the bedroom to check on them, Emmaline asks her to help move Petal onto the bed. Slowly and carefully, they pick up the barely breathing dog and place her onto the bed. When Emmaline lies down beside her, face to face, Darlene and Emmett leave. Darlene is surprised to see that all but Ruger follow them from the room. Once they're all quietly settled in the keeping room, she hugs each one, lingering on Jasmine, aware of what is inevitable.

GERALD IS IN THE FOREST with Day and Lolly, running as hard and as fast as he can. For over a month, he has felt Petal's slowing heart rate and her body's decline. There's nothing he can do. He knows today is the day that Petal will die. He has turned off the television because he was driving himself insane with worry and incessant thinking, searching the vast encyclopedias in his head for a way to prolong her life. He has read that Pit Bulls can live for seventeen years. He knows he robbed her, and Jasmine, and probably all of the other females of these extra years.

He feels weak as Petal's heart skips a beat. He stumbles and falls headlong down the steep hill. His body twists and turns, hits rocks and sharp nettles as he rolls uncontrollably downward. A large tree halts his tumbling descent. He rolls hard into it, his ribs hitting so hard against the trunk it takes his breath away. He lies still, unable to breath, needing desperately to breathe.

Finally, he can gasp little pieces of oxygen and then he's gulping the air. He remains lying against the trunk while he attempts to regain control of his body. He lies still, listening to his breathing and trying to feel his pain and discomfort but he's only able to experience that of Petal.

She leaves the world as she lived in it, gently, quietly, her eyes and thoughts on the one who loved her.

Gerald screams as loud as he can because he cannot cry anymore. He has cried enough tears for a ten million man army. His anguish is as real as his shame. Petal is gone. Jasmine is soon to follow. Then the rest of the females he neglected, used and abused. New Gerald acknowledges that he deserves every second of the suffering he's feeling. He wishes he did not. Yet if this is part of what it takes to keep him from ever returning to his past life, he'll take it, again and again and again and again.

"If it's necessary, old woman, I'll take it!" he grunts out as he lies in a limp heap against the tree.

Lolly and Day come near when they hear reason return to his voice. They put their damp noses on his forehead and lick inside his ears. Gerald reaches up and puts a hand on the backs of each of their big necks. They help him stand without having to be asked.

He looks into Day's eyes, eyes exactly like those of his mother. His coat is the same exact shade of gray. The white fur on his chest is the exact shape as Petal's. He doesn't know if he has her character and personality because he knows he never let Petal's develop as it would have naturally, if allowed to unfold in a caring, conscientious home.

He wonders if Day got his hyper alertness and guardian attributes from Petal. He wonders what she would've been like if she hadn't been chained to a steel post almost her entire life. He knows the females mostly like to lie around and be with Tiny. They don't leave her side unless they go outside to relieve themselves. Then it's right back to Tiny. If they had been given lives like Lolly and Day, lives which were appreciated rather than exploited, lives that were devoted to companionship rather than loneliness, Gerald knows they would have been so happy.

Even now, though he does feel their relaxation and peace, he knows Jasmine, Poof, Brownie and Harriet don't feel the carefree, exuberant joy that Petal's last litter experience. Nor do they have the bold confidence of her offspring. The girls are shy and retiring, waiting on Tiny to direct or lead. All they want is what was denied them their entire lives. They crave affection, companionship, concern, regard and comfort. Well, they have it now, and always will. A man changed makes changed decisions. A man who's slowly shedding a lifetime of evil can't help but be generous without desiring any sort of profit in return. Renewal is total.

TWO DAYS AFTER Emmaline and Darlene bury Petal in the newly formed cemetery beside the raised garden area, Emmaline announces she'd like to plant a tree in her memory. Darlene is seated on a chair in the keeping room working on lesson plans and nods her head slowly while looking closely at her. Her head stops nodding when Emmaline makes the next announcement.

"We need to go buy an oriental magnolia that has pink blooms. Where's the nearest plant nursery?"

Without saying a word Darlene rises, gathers her purse, and the keys to the most luxurious vehicle she's ever seen, and walks out of the house and into the garage. She opens the back driver's side door to let Emmett and Ruger jump in. She tosses the keys to Miss Emmaline who's shutting the door to the garage. She gets into the passenger seat, closes the door, pushes the garage door remote control, sits back and prays that Miss Emmaline will get inside the vehicle.

How she keeps her mouth shut when she gets in, starts the SUV, then backs out as if she's been doing it almost every single day, she will never know. Too scared to utter a word for fear it will cause her to change her mind, Darlene goes to work on the built in GPS system to program directions for the closest plant nursery. It's not until they're out of their subdivision and five miles down the road that she dares to look over at her.

When Emmaline looks back at her and winks, Darlene claps her hands and laughs out loud.

"Woohoo! We're buying a tree, you guys!" She exclaims.

Emmaline is laughing, too, when Emmett pushes Darlene's elbow to one side so that her arm falls around him. She hugs him close as they drive merrily down the road. The SUV still has the new car smell.

Weeks later, Darlene is in the kitchen organizing drawers when she comes across the envelope holding Miss Emmaline's identification documents. She peeks inside to confirm her find and spots her driver's license. Startled, she exclaims, "Miss Emmaline!"

Emmaline is standing before the range about to bring a spoonful of homemade vegetable broth to her mouth when the exclamation stops her.

"Yes? What is it? What's that?"

"It's your identification papers. You've been driving around with no ID! Thank goodness we haven't been pulled over!"

Emmaline has never possessed a driver's license. She had no idea how to get one and it never occurred to her to do so. She's beginning to think of her past as her primitive era. A dark time where she was ignorant of everything. In her time with Darlene she has learned a vast amount of knowledge she had no idea existed. The book knowledge is exciting. She's constantly fascinated by all of the information readily available to her. But what she has learned to value more than anything, is the civility, compassion, and generosity of spirit Darlene possesses.

Darlene has impeccable manners and an innate kindness in her nature. She's never rude, impatient or abrupt. She always thinks of others before herself and this does not diminish her stature, quite the opposite, it actually makes Emmaline admire and respect her more. For an individual who has known nothing but violence in all areas of communication, the civility and the indomitable strength it conveyed has been a revelation to her. Without Darlene realizing it, Emmaline began mimicking her table manners. She secretly watched Darlene as she ate or drank. She took notice of the fork or spoon she used, copied the way she held her knife when she cut her food.

One day, she and Darlene were watching a cooking show on tv, and Darlene commented that she thought the man had wonderful culinary skills but his poor etiquette detracted from it. Emmaline used the opportunity to suggest they get a book on etiquette and Darlene could show her everything the man was doing wrong. She had no idea what the word etiquette meant and she certainly had no idea what poor etiquette was. She did recognize, from the comment Darlene had made with an air of sadness and regret for the fellow, that etiquette was something valuable, something advantageous to know.

She recalls the etiquette lessons and games Darlene had devised. They'd both learned much from the books that were always mysteriously appearing whenever they mentioned interest in anything. She knew that Darlene thought she was the one ordering them, while Emmaline knew good and well that Gerald was listening in on everything, and probably watching, and it was he who was the continual benefactor.

As she puts down the spoon and extends her hand to accept the envelope, she thinks that driving without a driver's license is not only against the law, but that it's poor etiquette. She walks into the keeping room so that she can sit down and examine the documents at her leisure. When she's seated in the loveseat, with Ruger lying down at her feet, an always fatigued Jasmine on the cushion beside her, Poof and Brownie sleeping on elevated beds, and Harriet, stretched out beneath the coffee table, chewing diligently on a hoof, she places the envelope in her lap.

She hesitates before opening it. So much has happened, so many extraordinary experiences have come into her life. She glances at Darlene, who's squatting beside Emmett to change his collar from a green one with starbursts to a fire engine red with smiley faces. He's licking her face while she makes the change and Emmaline can't decide who has the bigger grin.

Darlene Cauley. A stranger, a tutor, a guidance counselor, her dearest friend. Emmaline is well aware that Darlene's salary, the bills for this home, the never ending deliveries of goodies for human, dog and garden come from Gerald. She has a hard copy of her monthly bank statement in the drawer of her bedside table. She knows that when the balance falls below four hundred thousand dollars, funds are immediately added to replenish and bring it back to that amount. What is he communicating to her with his largesse?

She removes her small plastic driver's license and reads every word and numeral on it. When she turns it over she discovers she's an organ donor. She's glad. She pulls out her passport and reads every page. She looks at her Social Security card and memorizes the nine digit number that is so critical to starting anything in a formal manner. She pulls out a white sheet of paper and reads the names of Petal's last litter of puppies and their spay/neuter dates. Emmaline had vaccinated and kept them on heartworm medication while she was with them. She reads they have all had rabies vaccinations and were given high dollar flea and tick prevention.

Somehow, she knows Petal's babies are still with Gerald, and that he's taking good care of them. She sincerely hopes he has learned what it means to enjoy and share the life of a companion animal, to appreciate their value, uniqueness, intelligence, and their mysterious ability to love unconditionally.

When she removes the final document and sees what it is, she's assailed with conflicting thoughts and feelings. It's her birth certificate. Her genuine birth certificate, not some forgery Gerald has expertly manufactured. She takes her time and slowly reads each word on the page. Her parents' names, Eric Jamal Carruthers and LaQuita Remarka Jones, are typed neatly in the proper boxes. She remembers her mother harping to her father that to help him remember to take care of his children they would have his last name. She knows now that a father should not have to be reminded he has children. That that's uncivilized.

She thinks back on the dark, profane ignorance of her childhood. Only after having spent those six peace filled, solitary months with her sisters, Ruger and Petal's babies, then living and experiencing the luxury of this home that had once been the not so foolish dream of a not so foolish girl, and then the education and friendship with Darlene, she has learned how human beings are supposed to, and should, treat one another and all of the other inhabitants of this planet. After learning and knowing that this type of graceful life is possible, she wonders why her family, her neighbors, everyone she knew in her past, why did they live such lives of sloth, hatred, violence, desolation and fear? Didn't they know that if you plant a seed and pour acid instead of water on it that it won't grow, but that if it somehow manages to survive it will be deformed?

She stops thinking about a past she can't change. She tells herself it is the past, leave it alone there. It's over it's done. To tarry there is futile. She looks up from reading and contemplating her birth certificate to take in her surroundings. She looks at the chic arrangement of the keeping room, the cool elegance of the kitchen, then her eyes travel to the window and behold a beauty she never tires of seeing, breathing and appreciating.

She recalls seeing the mirrored images of her surroundings. Someone used his or her brain to create something lovely, something soothing for mankind. Darlene has taught her that she has a powerful mind, that everyone does, and it can be used to create the good and beautiful, or it can be neglected and only take in the ideas of others, or worst of all, take in no ideas at all. That's what she was born into. She attributes the dereliction, the selfishness and laziness of her parents and extended family to guiding her toward a life of violence and abuse. It's terrible to be held in contempt by those who are supposed to love you. Deriding children is a death sentence for any culture in which the practice exists.

She has no knowledge of Darlene's past. She knows of her two daughters, but very little of her husband. An unspoken agreement was made that they would never ask one another personal questions. That they would concentrate on living in the present moment because really, that's all they had that truly mattered. She wonders about the upbringing of Darlene, how different it must have been from her own. She senses no deep pain or sorrow in her. She suspects something unusual and unjust must have occurred to bring a woman of such energy, skill and learning into the life of a broken, battered and uneducated individual. Maybe one day Darlene will tell her. And maybe one day she won't. It truly does not matter one way or the other.

GERALD COPYCATS TINY and enrolls in online university. He decides to explore other interests besides yoga, kettle bells and watching Tiny and Darlene twelve hours a day. He feels how excited Tiny has become. Her reading skills have advanced to above college level. Darlene ramps up the class time and homework. No matter how much schoolwork she piles on Tiny, and she piles it on like an Olympic gymnastics coach, Tiny rises to meet every challenge, then rises even higher as she aces all assignments and tests. She has become a vacuum of knowledge. Her brain is working all of the time, figuring out problems, reading book after book on a vast array of subjects, always seeking truth and mental adventure.

When Gerald began researching online universities, he decided to participate in the toughest, most elite programs he could find. He never thought he'd be glad he achieved a perfect score on his GED test he took at sixteen. It has proven to open doors without him having to fabricate fake grades and graduation certificates.

He likes that he can complete all of his work from his sofa or the kitchen bar, or from the front porch. That he never has to see anyone or speak to anyone because all communication takes place in online chat rooms and via email. He got out of video chats by submitting a forged letter signed by a genuine plastic surgeon stating he was horribly disfigured, his appearance known for distracting and terrifying people.

Problems do arise when the instructors refuse to allow him to complete the courses at his own pace. His professors will not give him a pass even though his attendance is perfect and his intellect startling. They won't make any exceptions, which Gerald finds tedious and ridiculous and stupid, and tells each professor as much. He determines he must forge documents, hack into networks and lie through his teeth if he is to proceed at his own pace. He has no qualms doing this since it's been his modus operandi since the second grade of elementary school.

He loses track of Tiny's progress as he becomes obsessed with his own. He determines he can complete an undergraduate degree and two master's programs in two years if he enrolls at six online universities. He enrolls in seven for insurance. He quickly learns that science subjects challenge him the most. Mathematics, logic, chemistry, biotechnology, microbiology and physics. These subjects hold and maintain his interest because the possibilities and discoveries are endless and mostly unknown. Like finance, there's no end, no finality.

His plan succeeds. By the time Tiny has finished her second year of college, he has his undergraduate degree and two master's. No score on any test or paper is below one hundred. He has yet to decide what to pursue when one morning he begins to feel a defeating, sluggish fatigue. Suddenly he becomes dizzy and there's an excruciating pain in his left ear. He thinks he's coming down with the flu when he notices Quantum stagger and fall.

Gerald jumps up from the sofa and gently lifts him to hold him. He immediately senses something is wrong in his inner ear. The twisting and tortured spasm disturbs him. He places Quantum in a small kennel with fresh clean towels on the bottom. The seizures continue and Gerald feels as though his ears and brain are on fire. He must use every brain cell he possesses to concentrate on getting himself and Quantum into Tiny's old SUV. His vision is blurred as he drives cautiously down the road on the way to the nearest animal hospital.

# Chapter 17

When he pulls into the veterinarian's parking lot he drives over a concrete curb. He has to fight to not stagger and crawl to the front desk. He's quickly shown to a room when the receptionist witnesses one of Quantum's body twisting seizures. When the young veterinarian enters, Gerald tells him,

"It's his inner ear. He's in a great deal of pain and has had three seizures in less than an hour. Your receptionist witnessed the last one."

"Office administrator."

"Excuse me?'

"She's the office administrator, not the receptionist."

"Are you going to examine my seizing cat with the inner ear issues who feels like his brain is on fire?"

"You have medical training in animal husbandry?"

"No, but I'm a qualified asshole, if that's what you need me to be in order for you to examine my pet who's in extreme pain. Second time I told you."

The young, cocky, inexperienced veterinarian looks at Gerald and is about to be a smart aleck when a creepy tingling on the back of his neck tells him not to. He turns toward the carrier and gently removes Quantum and begins examining his body.

Gerald watches him for two seconds before he says,

"His ears are on his head."

"I need to perform a complete examination."

"Could you start with his ears?"

Quantum begins seizing in the veterinarian's hands, causing him to drop the cat. Gerald's hands are beneath him, holding him safely before he falls one inch.

"Sir, the problem is in his inner ear. Will you proceed accordingly?"

The young vet is embarrassed by his clumsiness but has yet to be humbled by the trials and tribulations that will eventually melt and glue themselves to his life, defeating, enriching, and changing him. Instead of apologizing, he asks the vet tech to take the cat to be x-rayed. Gerald requests to be present for the procedure but is summarily denied with insubstantial excuses. If Quantum weren't in such pain, he'd insist. Neither the vet or the tech ask for his cat's name.

An hour and a half later Gerald is back home sitting on his sofa with Quantum sleeping exhaustedly and soundly on his lap. He's reading the printed sheets provided by the vet's office detailing their prognosis. He was overcharged, and their plans are to overmedicate his cat. The young vet thinks he covered his incompetency with prescriptions and a monogrammed white lab coat. He did not. Gerald's diagnosis, though imprecise, was correct. Quantum has vestibular disease.

Gerald hacks into the young vet's home and office computer system. He learns that the vet has dreams of owning a yacht. And he'll manage it if he keeps charging these prices and makes a serious effort toward learning his craft. He researches all ear related cases at the practice. He locates a ten year old file on a young healthy cat like Quantum that details the exact displayed symptoms and behavior. It doesn't, and can't, detail the pain he endured. The vet who made the report sold his practice last month to the young vet but has yet to collect his records, or maybe they were a part of the sale, which Gerald hopes so because the retired vet knew his trade and was a compassionate human being utterly lacking in frivolity, and the young vet needs the old vet's file like nobody's business. Gerald decides he does, too. He downloads all of the files to study at his leisure.

According to the file that is the same as Quantum's malady, the symptoms and pain should last twenty-four to forty-eight hours and may never recur. It should be allowed to run its course with no medication necessary. The vet who made the report charged thirty-five dollars, performed no x-ray and prescribed no medication. The young vet prescribed two medications, mildly sedated Quantum for the ten x-rays, then charged him two hundred fifty dollars for the pleasure of his lack of experience which ultimately exhibited itself as incompetency.

Rather than give into futile anger over the debacle, Gerald gives into decision. He decides to become a veterinarian. But not just any veterinarian. He'll be the most successful, the most skilled, the most gifted veterinarian in the world. And while he's at it, he'll transform the industry and practice. He doesn't know why he didn't think of it earlier. Perhaps because his background still slowed him down. But not anymore.

Between educating himself, listening and watching Darlene educate Tiny, he thinks that like Tiny, he's becoming a different person. Maybe not a good person, he knows himself well enough to recognize that may never be possible. But by listening to Darlene, watching the effortless grace, compassion and civility of the woman, he knows that the way they grew up is not normal. It was barbaric and backwards. It was the type of upbringing guaranteed to prevent success, any type of success in any endeavor. He also recognizes that the manner in which he and Tiny were raised is not only not normal, it was an aberration.

It's not normal to exist as a human being and live continually in predator mode, like him, or in prey mode, like Tiny. It's not normal to emotionally, psychologically and intellectually attempt to cripple every person who walks into your life. Normal is Darlene. She can make a delicious soup as easily as she can make meaningful conversation. She gives with no thought to receiving anything for herself. Gerald recognizes he's still incapable of that particular attribute of Darlene's character.

He's too interested in accumulating money and that particular character attribute would have slowed him down considerably. But Tiny has that. She always has. She has always cared for those in her life. Even when he was abusing her and allowing others to abuse her, she took care of him. His home, health, his dogs. He reckons some people are just made that way. He's glad he's not, because it'd drive him crazy. Gerald will never be the man in the room who'll turn the other cheek. He's that man in the room who will retaliate with consideration and then, without hesitation.

While Tiny finishes up the last two years of her bachelor's degree, Gerald obtains two PhD's online, in molecular biology and biochemistry. While he completed his PhD's, he also completed a degree in holistic medicine. He discovered acupuncture and decided to test its efficacy first hand. He still has pain in his hips. He finds several acupuncturists, but is disappointed when he does in depth personal, criminal and financial background checks. Only one meets a certain oblique criteria which Gerald seeks.

Twice a week, Gerald begins seeing Mr. Da, a nonagenarian Chinese gentleman who has practiced the art of acupuncture for almost a century, an art that has been practiced in his family for untold generations. Gerald becomes convinced of the veracity of the arcane art, and the skill of this particular practitioner, after only two visits. All of the pain in his hips and shoulders has completely dissipated. The first time Gerald asks for lessons, Mr. Da politely refuses. When Gerald came for his treatments with His Crew in tow, unleashed, yet perfectly controlled and behaved, Mr. Da was alarmed, then fascinated. A fascination that would eventually reward Gerald's future.

As Mr. Da inserts long needle after long needle into Gerald's supine body, Lolly, Day and The Lookalikes watch from underneath the table, and from various positions on the floor in the room. When Mr. Da told him dogs were not allowed, Gerald had said,

"Mr. Da, I don't know anything about acupuncture except anecdotal unverified stories. You may stick needles into me, but my dogs will watch you. If you know your profession, what's the worry. If you don't know your profession, they'll let you know. Shall we proceed?"

Mr. Da will admit to no one that when he saw the five huge, extremely muscled, but somehow elegant looking dogs walk into his clinic, he was terrified. More afraid than he'd ever been in his life. Everyone all over the world knows of the ferocious danger of the Pit Bull. Their reputation and stories of their reputations are unending, and always to be considered the absolute unvarnished unexaggerated truth. But once Mr. Da noticed the unquestionable calm and confident demeanors of the dogs, he relaxed, somewhat. He admits to himself that the situation is unusually intriguing. And at his advanced age, it's rare to find a genuinely intriguing circumstance. Yet, here was one presenting itself to him.

As he looks at Gerald's dogs lounging on his floor, not sleeping, fully aware, he recalls his first impression of this uncommon group.

This Gerald is by far the most beautiful human being Mr. Da has ever had the privilege of encountering. He would say Gerald stands two inches over six feet, and that his proportions are perfect. He has found not one fault on Gerald's body other than those made by man. If asked how Gerald is, what's he like, Mr. Da would simply reply,

"Gerald is flawless."

His medium to dark mocha skin is without blemish other than the surgical scars. His eyes are light brown with gold flecks around the outer edges. His thick eyelashes are hyper black in color. He has an aquiline nose, high cheekbones, a square masculine jaw and almost full lips. His black eyebrows are straight. If one were to take each feature on its own, they would not be remarkable, except for the eyes. But the manner in which they have been combined on this man's face, is uniquely spectacular. Mr. Da has never seen a human being so attractive.

Gerald has muscular broad shoulders. Mr. Da doesn't know if weightlifting or swimming has shaped them because he has the long lean tapered body of a highly trained swimmer. The big thighs, the slender buttocks. And he moves with the lazy elegance of a champion swimmer.

Gerald is lying on the wooden table while Mr. Da is seated on his stool just in front of his head. Gerald's eyes are closed and Mr. Da's eyes are half closed. This has become their ritual. Mr. Da applies the needles and once finished, Gerald pretends he falls asleep while the acupuncturist studies the large dogs.

He's struck by their demeanor, by the intelligence in their regard. It has been three months since Gerald began his bi-weekly treatments and still he cannot differentiate The Lookalikes. He will admit that Day, the gray and white one, makes him the most uneasy. He appears to be more muscular than the others, bigger, and most definitely the most thoughtful. Thoughtful? Can a dog be thoughtful? Can a dog even think? Three months ago he would've said absolutely not. Today, as he looks at these pets of Gerald's that he has observed, studied and never touched, he knows that indeed, these beasts think and consider everything they see and smell. It's fascinating.

Gerald, or The Gorgeous One, as Mr. Da secretly calls him, has referred to them as his companion animals. They look like warrior animals to Mr. Da. As he sits on his stool he contemplates the meaning of the English word companion, and then compares it to the behavior of these dogs and their relationship to their master. To be a companion is to be one who serves as a partner or friend, one who accompanies another, or one who is closely connected with something similar. He owns the complete Oxford English Dictionary and has read it for the past sixty years as one would read a novel. He's exquisitely aware of every meaning and nuance of the word "companion".

He studies them through half closed eyes on this day of Gerald's final treatment. He has accepted that these dogs are Gerald's friends. Dogs, it seems, at least these dogs, are more capable and aware of the meaning of friendship than most humans. They are also his protectors. And though Gerald would not admit it, they are his spiritual connection to life. He's still surprised at how clean and well mannered they are. How majestic. With their big blocky heads, their thick necks and chests, and all of those muscles that ripple across their bodies at the slightest movement.

He remembers his initial terror of them, the terrible rumors of the reputation of this breed. He now knows that it has nothing at all to do with the breed, but rather with the individual masters and mistresses of the dogs who make them do the terrible things for their own depraved pleasure and egos.

His eyes widen as he watches The Lookalikes rise one after another. They walk over and smell Day and Lolly underneath the slim raised wooden bed, then they go up on their haunches and put their paws on the bed so that they can look at Gerald. From his place behind Gerald's head he watches two of them perch on the right side, and then the other pure white female perch her paws on the left side. The two on the right look up and down Gerald's body at the long needles protruding from his chest and shoulders. The one on the left slowly moves her big head forward until she can smell the tip of one or two. Her nose almost touches the needle, but it does not.

Rain begins to fall outside and patter the metal roof over the small patio which extends from Mr. Da's work area. The three large white dogs stay exactly as they are, standing over their master, looking down at him as if he's the only human in the world. He will admit to no one ever how much these creatures enthrall him. He wonders how they came to be like this. The way they act, their confidence. He has never paid attention to any animal before, never given it any consideration, never imagined they were capable of this intelligent behavior he witnesses every time Gerald comes. He is ninety-eight years old and happy to report he's still capable of learning.

When Gerald asks him to teach him his craft, he's on the verge of saying no, as he does for every such request, but he realizes that if he says no, he'll never see these dogs again. These dogs who bring such an atmosphere of calmness and tranquility to his world. These dogs who have made him question not only his humanity, but his very existence, and without doubt, the appalling depth of his ignorance.

For the past three months he has had startling thoughts, thoughts that have changed him. When Gerald introduced the five Pit Bulls to him, announcing their names which marked their individuality and their uniqueness, Mr. Da secretly smirked at such folly. Americans and their pets! Such insanity! The way they let them in their homes, take them for unnecessary exercise, buy them collars, beds and special food. Why, it was lunacy! How much does it cost to feed these huge beasts? And if they get sick? They take them to animal hospitals! Who ever heard of such a thing! An animal hospital? Such a waste of time and money.

His thoughts regarding the pets are different now. He no longer holds them in contempt, rather he accepts each as a unique creature with unique characteristics and a unique personality. He cannot eat beef or pork anymore. He can eat chicken, but he feels his days are numbered on eating that creature as well.

Day and Lolly. The Lookalikes, which he cannot distinguish one from the other though he studies them and tries, unsuccessfully, to guess each week. He has failed each time and in his failure has begun to suspect that Gerald is changing the name tags to confound him. Last week when he accused him of such tomfoolery, Gerald made him lose face by calling each dog by name. It was clear he had guessed wrong when each pet responded decidedly to her name. Yes! Each pet responded to her name. The dogs knew their names. They knew how to stay, they knew what "No" meant, they knew what "Come" meant. They are intelligent. And he, though he will never admit it to Gerald, had eaten dog when he lived in China as a child. As he looks at their quiet, intelligent strength, he feels shame. How can it be that he is ninety-eight years old and just now learning that there is intelligent, interesting life besides that of the human being? Humans, we are so consumed with ourselves, he thinks sadly.

Last night as he sat on the floor with his family for their nightly meal, he looked at everyone, really looked at everyone. There were twenty of them seated at the long rectangular table his eldest son George had made. All of his children were given English American names so as to help them avoid bullying or teasing as they grew up.

George is short of stature like him. His hands are covered in callouses from his work as a carpenter who enjoys being much in demand. Mr. Da remembered when George had brought this beautiful table to his mother. He remembers being so pleased by its beauty and elegance. But when was the last time he recognized he son's worth? George is a hard working honest man. He is a good father. A good son. Mr. Da does not recall ever telling him that.

His wife takes care of his home, and him, with the precision and discipline of a military commander. He considers the room where they are eating, the delicious and plentiful food dishes sitting in attractive porcelain bowls she prepared. It's so clean and orderly. He notices for the first time how bright and beautiful the platters and bowls are. Where did she get those? They are lovely and present the food in an enticing manner. Has he ever expressed gratitude for her efforts and attention to detail?

His granddaughter, Lyn. He looks at her now, seated across the table from him. She has jet black glistening hair that is pulled away from her round face. She is smiling and laughing at some comment her younger cousin Sam has made. She is wearing silver earrings in the shape of cat faces.

"Lyn, why do you wear cat earrings?"

Lyn's chopsticks pause in mid stir. She cannot remember her grandfather ever directly addressing her. All conversation and noise dies to a standstill.

"Because I love cats, sir."

"You love cats? Do you have a cat?" Mr. Da is remembering that he ate cat when he lived in China.

"Her cat has three million followers on Instagram," says his grandson, Oliver.

He has no idea what Instagram is. But three million of anything is marvelous.

"What does your cat do to have so many followers?" He is so proud of himself for using the correct lingo.

"She's Kat, The Catiest Cat. She's really smart, really aloof and really insightful. From time to time she performs magic tricks."

"Magic tricks? What can she do?" Mr. Da is intrigued in spite of himself.

"She makes dogs disappear. And she reads minds."

"Reads minds?" A cat that can read minds! After having been with Gerald's dogs, he can believe it. "Why, that's wonderful!"

Lyn looks at her grandfather to see if he's making fun of her. When she's convinced he's not, she smiles.

"Not really, Grandfather. But she is entertaining when she pretends to."

And he watches his granddaughter grin at him in such a playful life filled manner that her exuberance somehow reaches across the table and infects him, and he laughs out loud. Then she's laughing and everyone else at the table is laughing. This wonderful hardworking family, who possess different remarkable skills, who spend hours upon hours working, then are expected to gather here each evening to honor the family. These are such good people. His family! Has he ever told any of them that he is impressed by their abilities and dedication? Have they ever laughed like this at dinner? No, they have never laughed like this.

He looks at his offspring, at their offspring, at his wife of over seventy years. This is a beautiful family. Beauty. This is what has entered his life through the visits of Gerald and his dogs. Beauty, wonder and awareness.

As Gerald is preparing to leave, Mr. Da tells him that he is thinking about getting a dog. Gerald is standing in the doorway about to leave, but he pauses.

"You don't need a dog. You're not a dog person."

"What is a dog person?" Mr. Da cannot help his sharp tone. He has been insulted.

"One who's not selfish. You only think about yourself. You don't think about anyone else. You're ninety-eight years old. And I think, too old and unwilling to change your ways."

Mr. Da looks at Gerald and is suddenly reminded of a king cobra. Beautiful, unpredictable, strong, fierce, and never to be underestimated. He has not encountered such a fascinating man in all of his many years on this earth. Or has he? And had he been too self-consumed to realize it? He decides then that he would be a fool to let this man disappear from his life. This man with whom he has never had a conversation until now, this man who has opened his eyes and mind to the beauty and wonder which has always surrounded him. Or does he wish the presence of this man to remain in his life because of what he witnessed earlier?

He remembers when he was watching The Lookalikes perched on the sides of the raised wooden bed. He wondered why they were staying there for so long when he looked down from their big heads and mighty shoulders to see Gerald's fingers and hands lightly petting their feet and lower legs. Though it is rare for Mr. Da, from time to time, he will allow himself to follow the path of his curiosity heedless of the outcome. He knows Gerald is to be feared more than His Crew. But a man who can effortlessly and silently control such formidable creatures simply by being with them, this is a man who is worth knowing better. He pushes his uncertainty and fear aside and says to Gerald, "I will train you in the art of acupuncture as I have trained no other before you."

Gerald turns to fully face Mr. Da and gracefully bows low in the deferential Chinese manner. He knows his gesture expresses more gratitude and respect than his words ever would.

# Chapter 18

From the kitchen window Gerald can see the profusion of colorful day lily blossoms in his circular bed in the middle of his lawn. The circle of lilies grows each year as he plants more plants, which he does when he discovers a color or type he doesn't have. He's thinking about the email he read this morning informing him of the third denial of his request to be allowed to take extra surgery courses. He knew he'd be denied. That email is a mere formality rather than a surprise.

He turns back to the screen which encompasses the entire wall between the two back windows of his living room. He watches Tiny and Darlene dig a grave for Brownie. She will be buried next to Harriet, who is buried beside Jasmine, who's buried beside Petal. He sees they have wrapped her body in a royal blue velvet bag. A wide off white satin ribbon is tied in a bow around it. Brownie, a beautiful long legged brown Pit Bull with a splotch of white on her chest, who was named Brownie by Tiny, not because she was brown, but because she was so sweet.

Brownie was the most docile and submissive of Tiny's family. She would've gone mostly unnoticed if Tiny had not made a devoted point of noticing her every day, petting her, saying her name to her, and doing the very best she could by her.

The women have marked off a large rectangle with gray granite stones for the cemetery. They've planted dark purple blooming oriental magnolias just outside the corners on the side farthest from the raised garden area. On the fence that marks the lower boundary of the cemetery, Tiny has planted fragrant pale peach rambling roses. Gerald knows they're fragrant because for the past two years he has watched her smell and savor the blossoms when they bloom. The women are in no hurry to bury Brownie. They dig slowly and steadily until there is a perfect rectangle perfectly three feet deep. They don't stop digging until precision is achieved.

He watches them lean their shovels against the fence, remove their gloves, then gently lift and lower Brownie's corpse into her freshly dug grave. Once finished, they put their gloves back on and begin refilling the hole with dirt. When this is completed, Tiny and Darlene retrieve a cardboard box bottom that's filled with large white magnolia blooms. They place the wide flowers one at a time on top of Brownie's grave until the freshly dug earth is no longer visible.

When this is done, they stand next to her grave and bow their heads for a moment. Then Darlene begins to sing.

Thus it has been for each of Tiny's sisters. Darlene did all the singing for Petal's burial service. But for Jasmine's service, Tiny began singing with Darlene, joining in when she could. Darlene sang hymns for Petal. Tiny sang Nina Simone, Aretha Franklin, Smokey Robinson and Cher for Jasmine. For Harriet and Brownie they sing hymns, U2, Marvin Gaye, Gregorian chants and children's nursery rhymes. What starts out as sadness eventually ends in laughter and peace. The singing lasts as long as it needs to. In three days, Tiny will place the engraved white marble grave marker Gerald will send. It will have the accurate date of her birth, and the lamentable date of her passing.

Gerald's thoughts return to the email. He has been attending veterinarian school for six months. He has, of course, surpassed his fellow classmates in everything. It has been a revelation to him, and his professors, the extent and depth of his innate surgical skills. He was as surprised as they were. Gerald is also surprised by his enjoyment of it. He likes helping heal the animals by using the least invasive surgical procedure possible. It's the curse of the old white woman that enables him to feel the exact location and the intensity of the pain or injury of an animal. Any animal he touches.

He knows Dr. Gordon Lubell is the reason he's being denied permission for extra surgical work and education. Dr. Lubell has been the head of the school's surgery department for ten years, and like Gerald, a professional asshole his entire life. Dr. Lubell will not allow Gerald to take extra courses because of what happened with the bald eagle.

Arriving at Dr. Lubell's class one day, the students were greeted with a living bald eagle. He was standing atop a heavy duty perch that had been hauled in specifically for him. The eagle was large and magnificent. His left wing drooped awkwardly from an injury. All chitter chatter had immediately ceased. The students had filed in as quietly as possible, unable to take their eyes from the legendary bird of prey.

The bird's handler stood close to his charge. Dr. Lubell, who looked like a Viking of yore with his thick wavy blond hair, perfectly trimmed beard and his offensive lineman build, had enjoyed the reaction of his students. He liked to keep everyone off guard because he liked to control - people, situations, everything in his orbit.

He failed to notice that Gerald only had eyes for the bird's injury. His brain was working rapidly, going over the vast storehouse of knowledge and research of avian anatomy. He studied the bird and his impeded movement. When he heard Dr. Lubell describe the surgery that would be necessary to correct and fully heal the renowned predator and symbolic representative of the United States of America, he asked a question without thinking,

"Can we examine the x-rays?"

Dr. Lubell, describing the imminent surgical technique to repair the bird's wing, not heal the bird's wing, was shocked not by the question, but by the temerity of a freshman student interrupting him. He had turned to seek out the offender and had felt the hairs rise on the back of his neck when he looked through the coke bottle lensed glasses into the unflinching, steely eyed stare of Gerald. There was something about this particular student that irked him. If Dr. Lubell had been more aware of his surroundings instead of himself, he would've recognized that it was not irksomeness he felt, but something he couldn't name because it was rarely a part of his existence; this something was uncertainty.

"Mr. Gerald, is it?"

"May we see the x-rays?" Gerald asked a second time.

"There are no x-rays. We'll take them prior to pre-op. But I can tell you from vast experience exactly what the injury is and how to fix it."

"You mean, heal it. That's what you meant to say."

If the room was quiet before, now it's as though they're standing in a vacuum. The students are young and easily intimidated and Dr. Lubell is a deliberate intimidator. Gerald intimidates just by breathing, and he's always deliberately breathing. The students have not attempted to befriend Gerald, nor do they ignore him. They've learned that he's their best ally and best resource, for just about any subject offered at the school. Gerald will tell them any answer and explain any concept when asked to. He does not try to be their friends. Gerald doesn't try to be anything. He's just the smartest human being any of them have ever met, and he's never been wrong. Not once. His gentle compassionate manner with animals has impressed them all.

"Young man, have you been listening to me? I've just explained the exact surgical technique that will restore its wings to one hundred percent working order."

"Him. He's not a robot, or any other sort of inanimate object. Him. I think you can avoid surgery by…"

"Mr. Gerald, are you an animal husbandry doctor? No, you are not. Are you an animal husbandry doctor who has years of surgical training and experience? Who has performed countless successful surgeries on all matter of animal, avian and reptile alike? And written five books on the subject? No. You are not so –"

Before Dr. Lubell can continue his self-important speech, Gerald has crossed the room and is calmly approaching the eagle. He's placing his hands on the bird's injured shoulder.

"What do you think you're doing?! Sit down!!"

But Gerald does not sit down, slow down or stop. His actions are so quickly executed that the eagle's handler had no time to react to the alarm in Dr. Lubell's voice. With one sure but gentle movement, Gerald snapped the eagles shoulder joint back into its socket. Whereupon the eagle stared eye to eye with his healer. He then carefully lifted both of his wings and stretched them to their full and glorious breadth.

Dr. Lubell quashed his displeasure and fury when he looked out onto his classroom and saw the open mouthed wonder, the awe, and the delight Gerald's actions had caused. Gerald had eyes only for the bird, and the fully restored movement of his wing.

Gerald is trying to be civilized about the repeated illogical denials. That's why he's in the waiting area of Dr. Lubell's office, where he has been waiting for over an hour. Gerald was on time for his appointment, the appointment time that was scheduled over an hour ago. His instinct is to believe that Lubell is deliberately making him wait in some sort of ill-disguised power play. It's not belittling Gerald, or making him aware of his place – which apparently is way below Dr. Lubell, and evidently, beneath his contempt.

Gerald considers leaving, is on the verge of leaving when he notices a familiar smell. He smells dog. It's not the smell of dogs passing through; it is the smell of one particular dog. He asks the plump brunette secretary, "Excuse me, Miss? What kind of dog does Dr. Lubell have?"

"Dr. Lubell? He doesn't have any pets. He says his schedule would be unfair to a pet. His love for animals is exemplified by the long hours he works to help them, and to teach you to help them, young man."

Gerald is nodding slowly, thinking that the secretary has heard that unnatural sounding spiel so many times that she has unknowingly memorized it. How many times would it take this blank faced middle aged woman to memorize something? One thousand, one million, one billion times? His dark musings are interrupted by Dr. Lubell's voice on the intercom asking the secretary to please show him in. The secretary smiles insincerely and without rising, gestures for him to proceed to his privileged audience.

Gerald stands and walks slowly to Dr. Lubell's closed office door. As his hand reaches to turn the brass door knob he notices a short black hair on top of it.

When he open the door and steps into the office, Dr. Lubell picks up his phone to either text a message or to pretend he's receiving a text. Either way, the disrespect is obvious and Gerald has grown tired of it. He looks closely at Lubell's desk, then at his dark blue tailored suit jacket hanging on the coat rack. He sees more short black hairs on the cuff and on the left sleeve.

Dr. Lubell notices that his ploy to demean Gerald is ignored, that Gerald is calm, as though he's been made to wait a mere five seconds instead of over an hour. He puts down his phone and says to Gerald,

"If you like my…"

Gerald looks at him and cuts him off by saying, "You have a dog in your home."

Dr. Lubell's perfectly tanned face reddens unnaturally and he insists, "No. I do not. I don't have the necessary time to dedicate to a pet."

Gerald continues looking at him, then nods slowly, and walks out of the office.

Dr. Lubell stares after his departing figure in confused frustration. It occurs to him that Gerald is taller than he first thought. There's something unsettling about that young man. He turns to his computer to research his records but his attention is averted when he receives a text informing him his shipment from Indonesia has arrived. His palms begin sweating at the thought of what this means.

GERALD IS SEATED in a midnight blue Mercedes-Maybach across the street from Gordon Lubell's pretender mansion. He's dressed in black from head to toe. He has a military grade thermal imaging device perched on the bridge of his nose. None of the tasteless homes, packed as closely as possible, are less than eight years old. In this neighborhood, it's all about the house, not what's living around it. His car is parked between similarly expensive rides along the curb. Gerald thinks someone on the street is having a party or a wake. Whichever it is, either the host or the deceased is very popular or very rich. Luxury cars, trucks and SUVs line both sides of Lubell's street from end to end.

Gerald is giving the house a thorough study with the thermal imaging device. He goes over the house from top to bottom but can detect no heat signature. He removes the apparatus to study the alleged architecture of Lubell's home. At first he thinks the three story structure sits on a slight hill, then he notices the cement block foundation is two feet above grade. Lubell has a basement. He puts the apparatus back on his face and focuses on the area of the basement he can see. He immediately detects a heat signature, though vague and not emitting much heat, it's there.

He focuses all of his attention on the form, trying to discern what it is. Whatever it is, it's lying on its side and not moving. He's about to exit the sedan when a big silver Range Rover pulls deftly into the garage. Gerald can see five human shaped heat signatures inside the vehicle. The large one of Lubell in the driver's seat, two small figures which can only be children, then two bigger forms seated beside them, which could be teenagers or adults.

When the garage door is completely closed, Lubell exits the car and opens the back driver's side door. Gerald watches the diminutive forms exit the car. He watches the two taller of the four hesitate, stop, then pick up the two children. Parents then. The taller heat signatures are the children's parents. He watches as they follow Lubell up the steps and into his home. He watches Lubell disarm his security system. He's still watching when Lubell gestures for them to sit on the floor, after which he jerks the two taller figures over and ties them up like calves at a rodeo. He speaks to the children, then repeatedly strikes both parents for no evident reason.

Gerald doesn't know if Lubell has rendered the parents unconscious or not. He suspects he has because they're not moving. His purpose has been accomplished though. The children sit down in complete submission and place their hands on their ankles so that Lubell can tie them up as well. The figures of the parents are limp but have vibrant heat signatures.

Lubell leaves the room, moving toward the back of the house. Gerald watches him stop, stand in front of a wall, reach up, then pull something down. When Lubell is descending the stairs into the basement, Gerald removes the thermal imaging device to replace it with another device appropriate to the situation. He grabs a black leather bag and smoothly exits the sedan.

He walks toward Lubell's ornate front door with purpose and confidence, as though he's an invited and expected guest. He opens the front door using the key he paid the homebuilder's drug addicted daughter to get for him. He leaves the door unlocked as he crosses the wall to wall ebony marble foyer. He pauses in the hall between the foyer and living room to turn every light on. When the lights reveal every corner and nuance of the massive room, he enters the space.

As he walks slowly beneath forty foot tall ceilings he takes time to look at everything, the subtle lighting, the expensive art hanging on the walls, the designer furniture, and finally, at the bound and gagged Bayus, a young Indonesian family who were kidnapped from their home by human traffickers because they fit an emailed description perfectly, and because where they lived was so overcrowded their absence wouldn't be noticed or missed. Rizky and Annisa are indeed unconscious. The children are so small and perfect they look like dolls. A boy and a girl, who look to be respectively three and four years old, both with straight silky jet black hair. Their terrified dark brown eyes watch Gerald as he stands over them.

The father's forehead is bleeding while the mother has a busted lip. Gerald looks them over thoroughly. He squats next to the tiny children and looks each one in the eyes for five seconds. Still in a squat position, he looks at the bruised and bleeding faces of their parents, at their bindings, then extra slowly at the manner in which Lubell trussed them up as though they were nothing.

Gerald stands and walks in the direction he watched Lubell's heat signature go. He enters a huge wood paneled study that's devoid of books. Each wall appears to be the exact same dimension, as if the study is a perfect square. Gerald moves toward the wall he saw Lubell go behind.

There's no doorway or any obvious evidence indicating it's a portal to a secret area of the house. He inspects the panel for any imperfection, indentation, something to show him how to open it wide. It's on his third inspection that he notices the short black hair. It's lying at a forty-five degree angle in the crook of the design of the wall panel molding. Then he sees it. On the left side of the molding there's a lever cleverly hidden and built into the molding. Gerald depresses the bottom and the top pops out. The wall opens slowly. When he looks back over his shoulder he sees the children staring at him with numb, frightened eyes.

Gerald turns back to the revealed hidden stairway and descends.

At the bottom of the stairs he discovers that the basement is half the size of the foundation of the house. Gerald does not pause in his stride but walks into the unknown, confident he will be able to master and exploit any situation he may encounter. A total lack of fear makes this possible. Fear is simply not a part of his genetic makeup.

Along one wall of the basement Lubell has set up a clinical work station. There are four large iron kennels. Along the opposite wall, Gerald sees four single mattresses on the floor. On the wall above them are heavy chains connected to the wall with manacles on the ends. The mattresses are not new, nor are they clean. There are no pillows or linens.

In the middle of the room are more large dog kennels. And like the ones Lubell is standing in front of, they're the heavy duty kind which look like little portable jail cells rather than places of safety and protection. He counts eight. Each has a large dead canine inside. Some are skeletons, some are skeletons covered in desiccated skin. They all have heavy duty locked padlocks on the doors.

Lubell is standing in front of a kennel jail that is against the wall next to his clinical paraphernalia. He's staring down at what's in the kennel. Gerald knows what "it' is. As he walks over to investigate the eight in the middle of the room, Lubell is so enthralled with his specimen or experimentation results that he isn't aware of anyone or anything else in the world. Gerald thinks he's also got the Indonesian family and the plans he has for them racing through his perverted mind.

His slowly scans the contents of each and every cage, taking in the lawless depravation of this man who has publically sworn to use his scientific knowledge for the benefit of society through the protection of animal health and welfare, and the prevention of animal suffering. It appears that Lubell is doing the exact opposite. When Gerald finishes his study of the corpses in the cages and the set up against the wall, he turns and walks toward him.

As Gerald comes closer to the locked kennels he sees inside one that there is a large Doberman Pinscher being deliberately starved to death. This was the vague heat signature he detected.

Lubell doesn't notice Gerald until he is standing right next to him, looking down at the champion bred black Doberman Pinscher that he's systematically, gleefully, starving to death. When he looks up at Gerald, it takes two full seconds before the look of gloating pleasure in his eyes turns into enraged disbelief.

"What are you doing in my house?! This is my house!! How did you get in here?!"

Gerald removes the glasses he was wearing which house a high tech UHD camera. He folds them to turn the device off, then places the glasses on the black soapstone countertop. Then he hits Lubell almost as hard as he can. Lubell responds by crumpling to the floor. Gerald turns to the cage pretending to be a kennel and looks at the motionless, barely breathing dog.

He removes the equipment from his bag and places it on the countertop six feet away from the cage. He plugs the machine in, takes a short USB cord from the bag and plugs it into the glasses. In less than eight seconds, Gerald has set up a television system. The images and sounds he has recorded since he entered the house show brilliantly on the white cement block wall. He connects his phone to the system in order to program the images to play in an unceasing loop. He can turn the device on or off, freeze frame or fast forward or make the images move in excruciatingly slow motion from any remote location.

He reaches down to Lubell and strips off all of his clothing. He retrieves keys from his pants pocket and his cell phone from his inner jacket pocket. He unlocks the padlock and opens the cage door. He removes one of his gloves and gently places one of his hands on the exposed portion of the big dog's head. He feels everything the dog feels, all of the suffering, all of the discomfort, all of the misery, all of the confusion, and all of the loneliness. He knows the dog feels the calm peace in his touch.

He puts the glove back on his hand and bends over into the cage to gently remove the once beautiful animal. He places him briefly on the pile of Lubell's clothes on the floor. He feels the dog's flicker of panic when the scent of Lubell is released from the clothing. Gerald quickly tosses Lubell into the cage, closes and locks the door. He removes the cell phone charger from the bag, places it next to the cage with Lubells's phone right on top of it. He knows he'll see it, that he can choose to call for assistance, but will simultaneously realize that the assistance will become aware of his crimes against animals and humanity.

# Chapter 19

When Gerald returns to the living room he places the enfeebled dog on a soft chair while he cuts the bonds of Lubell's human victims. The parents, consciousness returned, watch him fearfully. The mother is crying quietly because she cannot help herself. They watch as the exquisite looking man gently picks up the brutalized dog and walks from the room toward the front door.

Gerald is rechecking the comfort of his passenger, when Rizky and Annisa Bayu, cradling four year old Indah and three year old Budi in their arms, open the back doors and get into the car. When the doors are shut, he ignites the powerful engine, turns on the police presence detector and zooms away into the night.

Hours later, when Lubell awakens and finds himself naked and trapped inside one of his torture chambers he panics like the true coward he is. He rattles the cage door with all of the strength of his fury. He's about to scream for help when he sees the full color ultra high definition images on the wall. He watches in stupefaction as his secret life is revealed. His arms fly out of the cage to destroy the machine, to turn it off forever, but it's impossible to reach that far.

He sees his cell phone on the charging station right next to the cage and feverishly grabs it. He's on the verge of calling the police, the fire department, someone, when his finger freezes one millimeter from the touch pad. Sanity briefly returns. To save his life is to ruin his life.

Lubell sits back against the iron bars, his naked buttocks on the cold iron slatted floor of the cage. He cradles the phone in his hands as if it were the most precious item in existence. He begins thinking carefully, confidently, precisely, searching for a way out that will enable him to keep his reputation, station and wealth.

Ten years later when the gruesome room is discovered, Dr. Gordon Lubell's skeleton is still crouched in a corner of the cage with the cell phone cradled in his bony hands. The looping images have lost none of their bright and dreadful colors.

GERALD TEXTS DARLENE as he races down streets and avenues. He'd prefer to take the Doberman home but the women live less than five minutes away. Because he has instructed Darlene to keep her cell phone close at all times he knows she'll respond, and though it's almost one o'clock in the morning, she responds immediately.

Gerald is aware of every item in their household. He knows they have what's necessary to restore the dog to health. But they must begin proper treatment as soon as possible. This dog has been without food, water, exercise, stimulation, affection and care since he had the terrible misfortune of walking into the life of the esteemed head of surgery of the most renown veterinary school in the state.

Darlene is standing beside the metal mesh yard wagon in front of the front door when Gerald pulls into the driveway. She's wearing dog print pajamas with her stylish pageboy haircut mussed from sleep. Her once white roots that vied for supremacy over her bottle red dye, now rule the show, and her platinum locks look chic and sophisticated. The worried look in her eyes turns into alarm when she sees the state of the dog Gerald is carrying toward her. Her barest glance at Gerald awakens a long ago memory of being in the presence of the handsomest man she'd ever seen, however, her compassion and love for all living creatures moves her attention away from Gerald's beauty to the sack of bones covered in black fur he's gently placing in the cushion layered yard wagon. Darlene thanks him without looking at him. Gerald watches her caress the Doberman as she wheels him inside.

He watches her rereading his texts as she closes the door. He sees Emmett standing in the foyer quietly studying him. Black, beautiful, perfect. He looks like a rare and true champion. The door shuts, Gerald waits, thinking, dreaming, he lifts his hand toward the door knob, and, and... he lowers it and returns to his car, to a different future, to the rest of his life.

He drives the sedan down the pitch black three mile long driveway to his home. The Bayus are asleep in the back seats. The parents' faces are slack in an exhausted slumber while the children are cradled safely in their arms sleeping deeply, trusting. Something all humans stop doing as they age.

He pulls into the bottom floor of the big barn. The concrete fighting rings are gone. The chains on the walls are gone; they've joined the steel rods and other chains Tiny dumped in the bayou long ago. The walls are now high gloss white and shimmer in the beams from the sedan's headlights. Gerald pulls in between Tiny's SUV and his two tractors. Beside the tractors are the golf carts, four ATVs, a white Honda Fit, a silver Ford Focus, a Jeep and the various tools and attachments Gerald needs to maintain his property.

The Bayus are awake. Fear and trepidation have returned to their eyes and faces. Their shoulders hunch over their children in an unconscious protective gesture. When Gerald exits the car, so do they. He motions for them to follow him. They do so because following is ingrained into their behavior and natures. He walks to the room that was once used to house and forcefully mate the dogs during the fights. It's now filled with empty shelving units and six food filled freezers. Gerald points to the freezers, then motions for them to follow him once again.

He leads them upstairs to the lounge that now has inviting wide pine plank flooring. The only furniture in the vast room are two recliners, two sofas, two end tables and one large coffee table. He turns to what was once the bar but is now a full chef's kitchen. He remodeled it himself because he had time on his hands and wanted to see if he could do it. He looks at it now, dispassionately thinking,

"Yes, I did it. I can do anything I want."

After pointing to the remodeled sleeping areas and bathrooms, he leaves. As he descends the stairs he becomes interested in the thought he had and what the implications are: He can do anything he wants. Gerald mulls and massages this notion and by the time he opens the gate Tiny installed to the one acre yard she fenced by herself, he has made a game changing decision. The Qat Quartet rub on his legs in welcome while His Crew wiggle their rears and tails and grin at him conveying all of the joy they feel at his return.

EMMALINE AND DARLENE are on the covered back patio lounging in gently swinging hammocks as they sip sweet tea with fresh mint grown in their garden. They're watching Zeus and Emmett play hard in the back yard. Ruger is dozing directly beneath Emmaline's hammock. She has a bare foot hanging out of one side so that she can rub his thigh with the ball of her foot each time she drifts past him. Poof is sleeping on an elevated bed near Darlene's hammock, but not too close, because as Poof has matured, her superpower has markedly increased. Where once when she passed gas, it could only be smelled in the room of the occurrence, these days when she passes gas the fetid aroma spreads like a cloud throughout the entire home.

Poof poofs when she's awake and she poofs when she's asleep. The overhead ceiling fan, which is set on its highest speed, barely wins the battle against her potent gaseous excretions. Diet change, exercise change, no change has made any difference in her flatulent exuberance. Emmaline and Darlene don't complain. They've learned to keep cotton handkerchiefs in ziploc bags filled with dried potpourri harvested from their lawn and gardens. The bags are placed all over the home, multiple baggies on every surface. They don't mind.

Poof is the last of her sisters. Every time Emmaline looks at her, pets her, hugs her, walks her or bathes her, she's reminded of how Poof and her sisters kept her sane during an insane period in her life. Every time Darlene looks at Poof, she's reminded of when she first set eyes on her and the other Pit Bulls, how her life changed from hopelessness to wonder. She'll never forget the first time she saw them prancing through the garage door, one after the other, confident and beautiful. Exactly what she has become because of them and the tiny woman who was their master.

"Zeus is a miracle, isn't he?" Emmaline says out loud.

"You know what, he is. Look at all those muscles. He's so healthy. So alive!" says Darlene.

The women admire the beauty, grace and strength of Zeus. A Doberman Pinscher who was barely breathing when they met him, but who now, is running, leaping and wrestling on the green grass with Emmett. Two gorgeous, huge male dogs whose lives were changed because of a righteous, caring act.

"What do you think his story was? Why does someone spend thousands, because Emmaline, you know that dog cost thousands of dollars. Look at him! He's a specimen of the breed! He's almost as big as Ruger."

"Darlene, I can't figure people out. I will never understand purposeful cruelty. As long as I live, I'll never understand it. Especially against a creature who's at your mercy and who lives to love and serve you. To me, and I've given it some thought, it's utterly senseless. It destroys the victim and ultimately destroys all that's human in the perpetrator. When I look at Zeus running, playing, grinning, full of so much life and joy, my spirit is rejuvenated. I'm made more alive by his aliveness. Why do so few seem to fully understand the mysterious gift of companion animals?" Emmaline wonders.

"Doesn't the breeder check on the dogs they sell? I just couldn't bear not knowing where all the dogs went, what kind of lives they're living. I would have to know!" Darlene exclaims.

"I would demand regular photo and video updates. That would be part of our contractual agreement. I would also do a home visit no matter where it is," says Emmaline.

"Me, too! I'd require evidence of long walks, because that pure bred Doberman Pinscher is an athlete. Just look at him! If you get a Doberman Pinscher, you better exercise that baby."

"I couldn't be a dog breeder," Emmaline admits.

"Me either. Neither one of us could. We'd keep them all. We're only good at being dog lovers," says Darlene.

They swing and sip and ponder the world of dogs. Poof passes gas and they both calmly open the ziploc bags they have on their laps and breathe into them for a while.

When the coast is clear, they lower the plastic bags filled with dried flowers and go back to watching Zeus and Emmett.

"He's gorgeous. I love him," Emmaline says quietly.

Darlene promptly bursts out laughing.

"What? What's so funny?!" Emmaline demands.

"You are, sweet lady! You love all dogs, all chickens, all people! You're the kindest, most selfless, most loving human being I've ever met. And, of course, now, the smartest. Thanks to me."

The hammocks swing, the women laugh, the hummingbirds feed nearby, Ruger sleeps, Poof poofs and Zeus and Emmett play, play, and play.

Gerald breathes in deeply, comfortably. He turns off the big screen tv, shutting down his afternoon fix of Tiny and Darlene, and the way life should be lived. At the kitchen sink he rinses his glass and places it on the bamboo drain Rizky made for him. When he raises his eyes to the window he sees the Bayus working hard in their vegetable garden. Indah and Budi, now eight and seven years old, attend an elite private school in the city. He watches Indah gently admonish her mother when she thinks she's working too hard. She points to a low bench and then at her mother's huge pregnant belly. He sees Rizky, sweating, strong and content, observe the scene as it plays out. He sees the look of love in the man's eyes, and Gerald thinks how easy it is to be generous and kind. Deviant behavior, cruelty, takes much more time, planning and effort. He would know.

He could tell Tiny and Darlene all about the middle aged couple who bred Zeus, sold Zeus, had Zeus returned to them, then sold Zeus to Dr. Lubell. They sold Zeus and hundreds like him without a thought to their futures or existence. The fattening of their bank account was their only concern. They faked everything else.

When Gerald got home after delivering Zeus to his nurses and directing the Bayus to a home they could leave whenever they wished, he settled down on the sofa and went to work. He had not done deep background checks on his professors or any of the students because he was trying to be decent. That evening, he realized the decent thing to do would be to examine the lives of those closely associated with his own to see what they were up to. His first actions were to hack into the school record systems, Dr. Lubell's work and home computers, and Lubell's cell phone, which he'd cloned while he was in the basement.

He learned that Bert and Roberta Davis have been breeding quality Doberman Pinschers for fifteen years on the outskirts of Jarrettsville, Maryland. On their website are inspiring images of red and black Doberman dogs, along with erudite and convincing claims of champion bloodlines, assurances of health and fine temperaments. When he moves the cursor over the community tab, he learns they also rescue Dobermans from at risk situations. Even the at risk Dobies are stunning. They also vow that they keep up with every pup for the lifetime of the dog to ensure a loving environment is the order of the day. This is the first bald faced lie he uncovers.

Gerald combs through financial records, phone records and every single email. He sees a lot of money coming in, and no concern going out. He finds documentation indicating that Gordon Lubell has been a client eleven years running. He finds the initial contact email, his impressive application, then records of transfers of thousands upon thousands of dollars, and zero follow up.

Before he begins the total annihilation of the lives and futures of Bert and Roberta and their money grubbing breeding and "rescue" operation, he researches each individual who purchased a dog. He decides to take care of those who need care, and to publically humiliate, have arrested where warranted, everyone connected to the Davis Doberman Ranch. He does it because he can do anything he wants.

THE YEARS PASS and see Emmaline obtaining her doctorate degree in psychology. She also becomes certified in service animal assessment and deployment. She and Darlene start a boutique business that specializes in matching humans with an appropriate companion animal. It's part time, a labor of love, and because of this work they're able to prevent many animal related disasters from ever happening.

Gerald does exactly what he envisioned he would. He changes the methodology and business practices of veterinary service and animal care forever. After graduating first in his class one year ahead of his classmates, he opens his first Gerald Veterinary Services clinic. With GVS, he not only streamlines veterinary care, but he makes it affordable for people from all walks of life, and enjoys a hefty profit while he does it. He begins conducting half price spay/neuter clinics the first Saturday of each month, and soon, every Saturday of the month. When he approaches other veterinarians to join him, no one's interested. He's politely rebuffed each time he reaches out.

Within a year he has quietly and efficiently wiped out the spay/neuter business of every other veterinarian in the state. When GVS turns into a chain corporate entity, he does the same in every state. By the time he gets to Oklahoma, the fifth state, his reputation, the way he operates, and rumors of his infallible skill have preceded him. Oklahoma veterinarians are eager to join him and reap the rewards, both financially and in knowledge. The opportunity to work with Gerald and be advised by him make veterinarians leap at the chance to participate.

He writes papers on needless prescriptions of medications, and when inevitably sued by the drug companies for libel he sues in return. He gathers exorbitant amounts of evidence. The analyses of their drugs reveal the ingredients and manufacture, which are not only unnecessary, but downright dangerous and inhumane. The drug trials reveal even worse. His in depth research helps him locate the families whose pets died because of the money grubbing pharmaceutical companies.

It takes him one year in each state before spay/neuter laws are passed and enforced. Animal cruelty laws and the penalties become so tough that animal abuse and cruelty becomes a secret act one rarely learns of. He accomplishes these feats by reasonable request, then when that never works, he blackmails, publically humiliates, bankrupts, buys votes, whatever it takes to make it happen. And it does happen. Yes, it does.

After thirty-five years, thirty-five different states consistently report lower crime levels, a decrease in drug related crimes and addiction. In every state where companion animals are regarded with respect and admired for skill sets human beings will never have, the rest of The United States starts paying attention.

Law makers, elected officials, police forces and communities recognize a direct correlation in treating all animals in a humane manner somehow changes people and promotes positive progress and advancement in their local environments.

Little Indah Bayu is the individual who points out the difference GVS makes in whatever community a location appears. She's careful to not name him or her connection to him. She doesn't know how she would explain her connection to Gerald if anyone asked. Her parents still live on the second floor of Gerald's barn. It may as well be an apartment in Indonesia, as all of the furnishings and decorations reflect their culture, yet it's still way deep in a secluded area in the Southern United States.

Thirty-nine year old Indah reflects on her bizarre story. She doesn't remember the horror of her family's kidnapping or the monstrous intentions of the Viking man. All she and Budi remember is growing up in a huge house over a huge garage and storage facility. They remember the vast acreage in which they played, grew strong, and developed powerful imaginations. They remember the contented humming of their mother as she walked along a raised bench in the kitchen so she could reach the counter, stove top and sink. They remember wonderful meals, laughter, plentiful food, their own bedrooms and their own beds, always with clean smelling bedding.

They remember the wide smile of their father as he dropped them off and picked them up each day in a midnight blue sedan. They remember a peace filled life with huge Pit Bull dogs, who, as they died were replaced by other dogs, pigs, donkeys, horses, cows, chickens, guinea hens, peacocks, snapping turtles and more. Gerald would bring them home announcing them abandoned by their owners, or from abusive owners made to relinquish them.

She smiles now as she thinks of her parents and her twin brothers who continue to live happily on the second floor of the big barn and continue to take care of every needful one Gerald brings or sends to them. Her parents have never held jobs, yet they have never stopped working. She once told them they were Estate Managers and she loved the look of pleasure that came upon her mother's face.

As for Gerald, she doesn't think any of them have ever shared more than ten words with the man. And most of those words have been Thank you. Thank you for saving my family, for documents legitimizing our residence in America, for the year of intense private English lessons, for paying for the education of our children, for keeping us all safe, well fed, cared for, thank you for everything.

Any words with Gerald are rarer now as he's never home. He travels across the country, staying healthy with long hikes, and staying sane with camping trips deep in barely discovered forests, always with one or two happy and thriving foster dogs. Dogs deemed worthy only for euthanasia. She knows it won't be long before Gerald puts a permanent stop to that, too.

When Indah began her research on the impact of low cost spay/neuter and all of the other programs designed by Gerald to help companion animals and the people who took care of them, she had no inkling that such mundane, yet obvious, ideas and the disciplined implementation of them could change a community. But as she sits at her desk, with the spreadsheets, reams of pages of data all around her, her foster cats Lucy and Ethel dozing on the window sill, the information undeniably illustrates the results of his work and efforts. People need to know about this. People need to be made aware that when the lives of companion animals are valued, soon, all lives are.

She emails Budi her findings and tells him not to tell Gerald. He wouldn't like it. He likes to live quietly and anonymously. He doesn't like people knowing what he's doing. Yet Budi's position as Director of GVS operations demands that he know all of it. Really, she thinks, everyone on the planet needs to know.

WHEN GERALD IS SEVENTY-SEVEN years old he develops an uncontrollable tremor in his hands. He retires from surgery but not from travelling across the country in his camper managing his empire and personnel. He promotes those who are worthy, seeking out those who have an inclination and the necessary intelligence for clinical work, but could not afford to take the time off from work to attend university, and then vet school, much less afford it. The result is that he has the best and brightest working in the GVS system. The GVS conglomerate went international twenty years ago so he needs to constantly feed the business with good, honest, motivated individuals. How many people he sent to school and paid them while they went, he no longer even keeps track of them.

Budi Bayu and his three sons know. They know the numbers, all of the numbers regarding the minutiae of the vast workings of GVS. They have collectively grown the GVS brand in an unprecedented and unbelievably successful manner. Their ideas, followed by thoughtful actions, keep the business in a state of continual growth and expansion. Gerald knows the business he built from nothing into a multi-billion dollar international entity is in excellent hands. He has decided upon his death that Budi and his three hardworking, intelligent and compassionate sons, will inherit the entire GVS operations.

He's mulling over when to announce his retirement when he begins to notice an uptick of designer toy breeds coming into his Dallas, Texas locations. They have respiratory illnesses, cardiovascular deformities, vision and hearing issues, behavioral issues, the list goes on. One day he overhears two vet techs speaking in a breakroom. Gina Morgan, a young lady with great promise but from a defeated family background, says she knows where all these poor dogs are coming from.

She describes an unsavory family living in an unsavory area, but generation after generation breeding toy designer dogs that people still can't get enough of. His right hand begins shaking so much that he has to put it in his pants pocket in order to regain a measure of control. It's time, he thinks. Time for him to retire, time for him to pass on what he has built. It's time for him to go.

He walks into his office for the last time and removes his white coat. With slow, concentrated movements, he hangs it on a hanger, puts it on the rod, closes the closet door, and leaves the office forever. He will never return, never be seen in this city or state again.

# Chapter 20

Little Cougar is lying down on her bed beside his desk. When he walks out, so does she. Little Cougar is not called Little Cougar because she's little or because she's a cougar. She's a Great Pyrenees/Anatolian Shepherd mix weighing one hundred and fifty pounds. She has bright ice blue eyes, eyes she has only for Gerald, who became her master when she was twelve weeks old. She was a small soft ball of beige, white and brown fur hiding more fleas than he'd ever seen in his life. She was found in a rice bag in the garbage can behind a Korean restaurant.

A garbage man happened to see the bag move and cared enough to look inside. She had immediately attacked him. He had brought her to the nearest GVS clinic. Everybody knew the reputation of the GVS clinics, that they helped animals no matter what. Gerald remembers the day the big garbage truck barreled into his parking lot.

Sick, emaciated, covered in fleas and still full of fight. She wouldn't let anyone touch her but Gerald. Three years later, she still won't. She still bites, still has plenty of the vicious in her, and she's always with him. Gerald considers this giant, elegant, moody beast his soul dog. She has been known to pitch screaming fits when she can't find him.

When Gerald opens the door to Tiny's beat up SUV, she jumps in like she always does. He turns the key and the motor rumbles to life. He thinks he's on the fifth motor and the third paint job. The seats are pretty uncomfortable, but Gerald doesn't like to drive anything else.

He drives straight to his destination. He knows the area and the neighborhood. He shut down two dog fighting rings near here years ago. It's a bad place where bad things are always happening. They can't seem to help themselves. To get to the reputed locale of the toy dog breeding facility he must drive down a rutted gravel road that floods whenever it rains hard. When he's a mile down the road, he thinks he knows exactly which place it is.

A long red brick ranch style home with green architectural shingles on a hip roof sits one hundred feet back from the road. The yard needs mowing, and while they're at it, they should haul off the six rusted, dilapidated and discarded autos littering the front and right yard. In the back yard, he sees a long building that must have once served as a commercial chicken coop. There's a vague overgrown road on the right that runs down the length of the property. Gerald drives down it like he owns it.

The back of the house is much worse than the front. There's zero pretense of order and decorum here. The eaves are rotted, the rear roof slope has a different type of shingles on it and it's so patched and missing so many shingles that he's positive it leaks. Plus the huge blue tarp nailed to the roof tells him as much. One corner is loose and flapping in the wind, the metal grommets slamming repeatedly against the exposed water stained plywood roof decking.

He sees broken windows, four foot tall grass sprawling wherever it can grow. Rusted appliances laying on their sides, broken toys and wheelless bikes, trash and debris strewn all over the place. The people who live here must navigate a maze in order to reach the extra large above ground pool with the brand new ten foot deep deck encircling half of it. The old chicken coop is fifty feet from the aquatic fun area. Gerald drives right up to the front door of it.

It's the beginning of so called autumn, but the temperature is in the low nineties. He rolls down all of the windows in Tiny's SUV and turns to tell Little Cougar to get in the back and lie down. Before issuing this command, he gives her another, more important one. Gerald places one steady hand on her furry neck, looks her in the eyes and says,

"If you hear any trouble, you come get me, girl. Now get on in the back and lie down. Stay low, unless you hear something."

Little Cougar, one hundred fifty pounds of pure muscle, loyalty and barely controlled wrath, licks the left ear of the one she loves with her whole heart before she obeys his instructions. Gerald exits the SUV and steels himself for what he is about to see, and for what must be done. He can smell death before he slides back the rusted corrugated aluminum door. He has imagined what he will see, but the utter depravity of the sight is beyond even his jaded comprehension.

There's a twelve foot wide dirt alley running down the entire length of the building. On either side of the dirt alley, where once chickens were forced to live in jam packed degraded circumstances that were outlawed five years ago, there are metal enclosures which are four feet wide and six feet deep. There are red oblong plastic buckets attached to the front of each cage. Beside the red bucket is a clear plastic one, similar in shape and length. The red one is for food, the clear one for water. In practice, the containers are filled once a week and the prisoners have food and water for the entire week.

As he walks down the alley he sees the water is green with algae growth and the algae has blocked the flow of water from the nozzles. He looks into the wire enclosures and sees years of neglect. There are piles of feces three feet high. There are tiny little dogs whose fur is so matted, some can't see, and some can barely move. Their coats are so packed with filth and debris he has no idea what their true colors are. He sees a tiny dog lying on the corpses of other tiny dogs because it's that or the feces.

He reaches over into one enclosure to pick up a three week old puppy. He sees maggots feasting on her rear end.

There are hundreds and hundreds of Yorkshire Terriers, Chihuahuas, both long haired and short, Pomeranians, Maltese, Shih Tzus, Miniature Pinschers, Tea Cup Poodles, miniature Dachshunds, and toy Fox Terriers. All are so inbred it's a malevolent wonder that any of them are alive.

He's ripping an empty water container from the front of the cage to cut it in half so that he can put the puppies inside it and at least save them today. He feels the spirit of the one he's holding leave her tiny little body when six morbidly obese human beings waddle ferociously into the coop of horror.

Gerald is gently placing the corpse of the puppy on the ground outside of the cage when the fattest of the six demands,

"What do you think you're doing here!? Who are you?! This here is private property. Mama! There's some old black dude trespassing on our property!"

Gerald notices the fat woman is without fear, shame or regret. An image from a long ago familiar day comes to his mind. He straightens slowly and turns to face the gelatinous mob.

There are  three women and three men. He sees an older woman, just as fat, if not fatter, slowly bringing up the rear. He watches as she pushes though the disgusting corpulence of her sons and daughters. She plans to aggressively confront him, to threaten him, and if at all possible, to physically harm him. But when she comes face to face with this tall, exquisitely formed old black man, she hesitates. And in her hesitation, her moment of pause and clarity, she feels something she hasn't felt in over half a century. She feels fear. Deep, involuntary sphincter tightening fear. Show stopping, threat killing fear.

She turns to her sons and daughters for support but they're out of breath from the exertion and the rare moment of excitement. She sees also, that like her, they have sensed something very dangerous in this man.

The one who speaks is Gerald, looking at each and every one as he utters the words once said to him,

"From this moment on, you will feel everything these companion animals feel. You will feel their pain, their discomfort, their confusion, their anxiety and their fear. You will feel and smell the filth and squalor you force them to exist in against their wills. If you kill them, you will feel it every year on the day at the exact moment of his or her death for the rest of your lives. And if you continue to breed them, you will feel them all. All of them, from every puppy mill and back yard breeder of toy designer dogs in the world. If you get rid of them, you will still feel. If they are killed by another, you will still feel. If they are abused by another, you will still feel. As of this moment, all of you are forever connected to these extraordinary creatures you have enslaved and imprisoned in this unnatural existence of filth, squalor, sickness and terrified submission.

When the last word of the old white woman's curse leaves Gerald's lips, he feels as if the weight of the world has been lifted from his shoulders and spirit. He walks past the stunned and silent grossly overweight family. As he walks past the fattest female, from the corner of his eye, he sees her begin to scratch herself all over. When he has closed the SUV driver's side door, he sees them in the dirt alley slapping away imaginary flies and insects they believe to be swarming all over them causing the nonstop stinging from little tiny teeth. He sees dark brown stains begin to form on all of their rear end areas.

As he reverses the vehicle, he watches two of the men run as fast and as best they can toward the above ground pool and throw themselves over the side into the cool water. But the water offers no refreshment and no reprieve. They hurt, they ache, they will suffer, but like him, hopefully, they'll figure it out eventually. When he comes to the gravel road, he stops to text someone who knows everyone.

By the time he has driven down the rutted gravel road and is turning onto the highway, one police patrol car, one sheriff's SUV, one animal control truck, three television vans and two rescue vans have sped past him. There will be quite a crowd, an uproar of epic proportions, arrests, and inevitably, changes. Because no matter that it seems as if the human race is descending into barbaric behavior and blissful ignorance, the exact opposite is true. The human race is progressing in the right direction, towards humane living conditions for all, to rehabilitating the planet, towards an enduring existence where compassion and thoughtfulness will be the order of the days. It may seem like it's taking forever, but maybe that's the way it's supposed to seem.

Gerald drives slowly home. Little Cougar sits on the floor in the middle between the two front seats. She's leaning against the one she loves with her whole heart because she senses he needs it. Gerald is quiet and thoughtful as he drives. Slowly, he becomes aware of a new sensation coursing through his body. At first, he doesn't understand it. He wraps his arm around Little Cougar to see if he still has the curse that blessed his life and the lives of countless others. It's still with him. He's acutely aware of everything she feels. It brings him peace.

Peace.

This is the foreign sensation he can now name. For the first time in his life he is at peace.

When he turns onto his street he sees a bright red Porsche Cayenne parked in his driveway.

"That looks just like the one I bought for Miss Emmaline Carruthers last year, Little Cougar."

It looks like hers because it is hers. He sees the two deaf white Pit Bull puppies he deposited at her front door two years ago. They're big and curious and grinning and hanging out of the driver's side passenger door window.

Dr. Emmaline Carruthers, published author, marathon runner, master gardener, companion animal rehabilitator, and most recently, full time foster mom to Darlene, a one eyed three legged arthritic light tan senior Chihuahua who's seated in the passenger seat wondering where on earth she is, whose car it is, who the sweet little black woman is, the senior Chihuahua who's staring in gentle confusion at everything because she has advanced canine dementia. Human Darlene would've loved her namesake, the umpteenth in a long line of foster dogs whom Emmaline has welcomed into her life and home since Darlene passed from this existence into the next. She always has a dog named Darlene as a constant reminder of her dearest friend. The woman who taught her to be happy, giving, awake. The woman who taught her to always be trying to do something good for another. Darlene, the who taught her, and Gerald, how to be human beings.

Gerald looks at the woman he has spied on through both the lenses of hidden cameras and other shadow devices. This woman he has spied on with his own two eyes as she graduated from college and accepted her undergraduate, master's and finally the diploma for her doctorate as strangers in an auditorium applauded her accomplishments. This woman he watched time after time cross many a finish line as she ran designated miles for many a good cause.

She is as beautiful as she was the very first time he saw her, when she turned in her seat in the classroom to smile at him, and welcome him to her school.

The timidity she possessed then is gone. Here is Tiny, Emmaline Carruthers, standing as tall as her height will allow. Confident, sure, living a life filled with purpose and unmistakable direction. She reaches through the rolled down passenger window and pets Little Cougar, who does not try to bite her, but who instantly obeys her when she opens the door and asks her to hop into the back of the Cayenne.

Dr. Emmaline Carruthers walks around to his driver's side door, opens it and extends a steady, but lightly calloused hand toward Gerald.

He wants to look away, but he can't. He takes in her trim form, her smooth unblemished, barely wrinkled skin. He can smell lavender and something else. She's wearing a pink linen shirt and form fitting faded jeans. Her sneakers have embroidered flowers on them. The diamond faced Vacheron Constantin watch he sent her for her fiftieth birthday is on her left wrist. She wears no other jewelry than her smile. A smile that is both sincere, and beckoning.

"Come on, Gerald. It's time for you to come home."

Gerald slowly extends a trembling hand toward her, which she takes in her firm grasp. As they walk hand in hand to her car he knows the moment isn't romantic, that she's here to help him because he has difficulty helping himself. And as he holds her little hand in his and feels the joy and contentment she feels, he sighs deeply and accepts the newfound peace as the one he loves with his whole heart leads him wherever she will.